John's Patmos Encounter

Its Relevance for Today's Christian

2

John's Patmos Encounter

Its Relevance for Today's Christian

The Rev. B. Lee Ligon-Borden, Ph.D.

Ekklesia Publications

Frisco, Texas

John's Patmos Encounter
Its Relevance for Today's Christian

ISBN 978-0-9889552-5-7
© B. Lee Ligon-Borden, Ph.D., M.A., M.A., M.A.R.

Published by
Ekklesia Publications
P. O. Box 5343
Frisco, Texas 75035

Printed in the United States of America

Books may be purchased through Amazon or Ekklesia Publications.

Unless otherwise noted, Scripture taken from the New King James Version ®. Copyright © 1982 by Thomas Nelson, Inc. Used by permission. All rights reserved.

ALL RIGHTS RESERVED

No portion of this book may be reproduced, stored in a retrieval system, or transmitted in any form or by any means, including electronic, mechanical, photocopying, recording, or otherwise, without prior permission from the author or publisher. The only exception is brief quotes in printed reviews.

For Gordon
my best friend

6

ACKNOWLEDGEMENTS

No one produces a book alone. Whether acknowledged or not, many people enter into the development of one's perspectives and approaches. Such is certainly the case with this book. Indeed, so many people have been involved in the process of getting these messages from the typewriter (yes! I used a typewriter for the first version, so that should give some of you some idea of what's been involved) to this stage that I cannot possibly name all of them. You know who you are and that I am grateful for your influence on my life. Certainly, I am grateful for my children, who were completely underfoot back in the typewriter-version days but came through marvelously when it needed to be proofed. Since those days, they have blessed my life with four spouses and ten grandchildren. Thank you!

For this recent version, I thank my husband Gordon, first of all, for all of his scholarly input, especially with the Greek, and for his unwavering patience and encouragement. His expertise in the kitchen and with dog pampering increased exponentially as the book progressed. I thank my dear "adopted Mama," who has been a role model for the "faithful servant." I also thank my friend and colleague, Fr. Link Hullar, for his encouragement and for his prayers for this project. Always, I am grateful for my bishop, the Rt. Rev. Dr. Bill Atwood, for his spiritual oversight and for all he has meant to me, my family, and my ministry – more than he can know. To all of you and to others not named, I am deeply indebted.

Table of Contents

PREFACE: A BOOK LIKE NO OTHER 13

"THE REVELATION"

CHAPTER ONE: "THE REVELATION" 17
- APOCALYPTIC 17
- DISTINCTIVELY DIFFICULT 18
- UNIQUE 19
  - *The "Sender"* 19
  - *The Recipients* 20
  - *Authority* 21
  - *A Warning!* 21
  - *The Promise* 22
  - *Embedded Letters* 23

JOHN'S SALUTATION

CHAPTER TWO: JOHN'S GREETING 27
- GRACE 27
- PEACE 31

CHAPTER THREE: JOHN'S DOXOLOGY 33
- THE FATHER – *I AM* 33
  - *Eternal Existence* 33
  - *Omnipotence* 34
  - *Love* 35
- THE SPIRIT – HIS COMPLETE SUFFICIENCY 40
  - *"The Spirit of the Lord"* 41
  - *"of wisdom and understanding"* 42
  - *"of counsel and power"* 44
  - *"of knowledge and fear of the Lord"* 46

THE SON – HIS REIGN AS WITNESS, FIRSTBORN, RULER	47
Faithful Witness	*47*
Firstborn from the Dead	*49*
Ruler of the Kings of the Earth	*50*
HIS PEOPLE – THREE TRUTHS CONCERNING THEM	52
Loved by Christ	*53*
Washed in His Blood	*55*
Made His Priests	*57*
CHAPTER FOUR: HE IS COMING	**59**
COMING WITH CLOUDS	59
EVERY EYE SHALL SEE HIM	64
ALL THE TRIBES WILL MOURN	66
THE ALPHA AND OMEGA	66

JOHN'S NARRATIVE

CHAPTER FIVE: JOHN'S STORY	**69**
THE BACKGROUND	69
Family Bond	*69*
Tribulation	*70*
The Kingdom	*72*
Patience	*73*
SETTING AND SITUATION	74
CHAPTER SIX: A DAY TO REMEMBER	**77**
IN THE SPIRIT	78
THE LORD'S DAY	82
VOICE LIKE A TRUMPET	84
Old Testament Instances	*84*
Jesus Christ's Second Advent	*85*
CHAPTER SEVEN: INSTRUCTION	**89**
WRITE IT: THE MESSAGE	89
SEND IT: THE RECIPIENTS	93

ONE LIKE THE SON OF MAN

CHAPTER EIGHT: THE GLORIFIED CHRIST 99
   A FIGURE APPEARS 99
      The Lampstands *99*
      His Garment *101*
   HIS PHYSICAL APPEARANCE 103
   JOHN'S REACTION 104

CHAPTER NINE: CHRIST'S RESPONSE TO JOHN 109
   THE TOUCH 109
   SEVEN WORDS 110
      "Fear not" *111*
      Six "I Am " Statements *112*

CHAPTER TEN: JOHN'S COMMISSION 121
   CHRIST'S EXPLANATION 121
   JESUS CHRIST'S PRESENCE IN THE CHURCH 124

AFTERWORD 125

PREFACE

A Book Like No Other

Of all the books of the Bible, none holds a greater element of wonder and mystery than does Revelation. Besides being distinctively difficult to understand, the book has several unique elements that we will consider as we go along.

Considerable scholarship has been devoted to theological exegeses of the text or to symbolic implications or parallels to other Scriptures. This book takes a different approach. It is intended to provide a practical and devotional consideration of how the truths contained in the first chapter – John's encounter with the risen and glorified Lord Jesus Christ – is relevant to our lives as 21st-century believers. Certainly, what the risen Christ had to say some 2000 years ago to His Church should have bearing on our personal spiritual journeys. Perhaps this book will help illuminate some of the ways in which we can apply those words to our lives.

It is my hope and prayer that the Lord Jesus will be pleased to have its relevance for today put in this form. If there is any error, it is, of course, solely mine. If there is any blessing, then all honor goes to our Lord God.

Shall we move forward now in our efforts to search out what the Lord has for *us* as we venture an attempt to grasp principles from John's Patmos encounter?

The Rev. B. Lee Ligon-Borden, Ph.D.
May 2016
Colossians 1:18

"THE REVELATION"

Apocalyptic
Distinctive
Unique

The Revelation of Jesus Christ, which God gave Him to show his servants – things that must shortly take place. And He sent and signified it by His angel to His servant John, who bore witness to the word of God, and to the testimony of Jesus Christ, to all things that he saw. Blessed is he who reads and those who hear the words of this prophecy, and keep what is written in it; for the time is near.
(Revelation 1:1-3)

CHAPTER ONE

"The Revelation"

The Revelation of Jesus Christ, which God gave Him to show his servants – things that must shortly take place. And He sent and signified it by His angel to His servant John, who bore witness to the word of God, and to the testimony of Jesus Christ, to all things that he saw. Blessed is he who reads and those who hear the words of this prophecy, and keep what is written in it; for the time is near.

The Revelation is a narrative – a story. It is John's story of his encounter with the risen and glorified Jesus Christ, and it includes instructions for writing letters to seven churches and an account of strange things to take place in the future. It is more than a mere narrative, however; it is apocalyptic, fraught with difficulty, and unique. We will look at these three characteristics briefly before getting into the narrative itself.

Apocalyptic

First, it is a "revelation" (note, it is not RevelationS, plural, as people often call it). The Greek word is *apokalupsis*; the transliteration is *apocalypse* and means an "uncovering" or "unveiling," usually of something that has been hidden or concealed. It is used in the New Testament most frequently to refer to divine truths previously unknown and incapable of discernment apart from divine revelation.[1] For instance, Paul uses it regarding "the mystery" or purpose of God in this age,[2] the mind of God for the instruction of the Church[3] and for His guidance,[4] the future glory,[5] and Christ's return.[6] The singular term "revelation" indicates the importance of viewing the book as

---

[1] Ladd, p. 19
[2] Romans 16:25, Ephesians 3:3
[3] I Corinthians 14:6, 26
[4] Galatians 2:2
[5] II Thessalonians 1:7
[6] Romans 8:19

a whole, for it emphasizes that "it is *the* Revelation—one . . . continuous manifestation of God's unique Son, the anointed Prophet, Priest, and King."[7] The literary figure Sir Walter Scott explains that

> The word "Revelation" gives unity to the many and diversified communications, whether in word or vision, contained in the book. Revelations there were, but these form one compact whole, and this belongs to Jesus Christ.[8]

So, we have God unveiling a truth or truths.

Are we willing to listen and respond?

Distinctively Difficult

This text is distinctively difficult in several respects. Certainly, no other book of the New Testament is so often misunderstood, ignored, questioned, or even disdained by students of Scripture. The book is said to "fascinate and also perplex the modern reader" and to be "the most obscure and controversial book in the Bible."[9] Morris Ashcroft observes that Revelation is not only "the strangest book in the New Testament," but that modern readers either ignore it or, worse, misuse it."[10] Likewise, Leon Morris notes that the book is "by common consent, one of the most difficult of all the books of the Bible" and, consequently, "remains for the most part a closed book."[11] For these and other reasons, many people avoid it.

Further, it is almost exclusively prophetic. Walvoord notes that it

---

[7] Ironside, p. 9
[8] Scott, Revelation, p. 18
[9] Johnson, 399
[10] Ashcroft 240
[11] Morris 14

is in many respects the capstone of futuristic prophecy of the entire Bible and gathers in its prophetic scheme the major themes of prophecy which tread their way through the whole volume of Scripture.[12]

In conjunction with its prophetic nature is the considerable use of symbolism.

Unique

The Revelation also has several unique aspects. I use the term *unique* because all of the Revelation, not merely the Letters, is different from any other book or epistle in the Scriptures in many respects. It stands alone in emphasizing the risen and glorified Christ. We'll look at a few of these aspects briefly as those differences pertain to us.

It stands alone in emphasizing the risen and glorified Christ.

The "Sender"

One unique aspect is that the message comes directly from the crucified, risen, and glorified Lord Jesus Christ, who tells John, as we shall see, to write it all down. Everything else we have directly from Jesus – such as His teachings, His rebukes, and His prayers – are recorded in the Gospels and the first part of Acts. Only a small portion of those texts deal with events that took place after the Resurrection, and in none of them does He give specific instructions to "write down" what is about to be revealed. Hence, this message must be very important if the Lord Jesus left heaven and appeared to John to reveal it. John was faithful in recording it –

Will we be faithful in heeding it?

---

[12] Walvoord, p. 23

The Recipients

It is written to a specific audience, namely the servants (Gr., *doulos*) of Jesus Christ. It is for those of us who have come to God by faith in Christ's finished work on our behalf and have become His followers.

Doulos implies much more, though, than merely a response to Jesus or being "saved." In ancient Greece, the word was used for a slave, and even though it often is translated as *servant* or *bondservant*, *slave* is really a more appropriate vernacular rendering. We are reminded of Paul's words to the Corinthians, "You are not your own, for you were bought at a price"[13] or his admonition to the believers in Rome to offer their "bodies as a living sacrifice, holy and pleasing to God."[14] The Amplified Bible expands the passage in I Corinthians to say that it refers to those who were purchased and paid for and made His own.

> *Taking the name of Christian means that one is more than a mere "fan" or "groupie." It requires more than being a mere spectator. A commitment is involved.*

There is more: it refers to those who want to follow Christ. Taking the name of *Christian* means that one is more than a mere "fan" or "groupie." It requires more than being a mere spectator. A commitment is involved. It is not for those who are merely "curious" or "convinced," but for those who are "committed."[15] So, the question is, do we recognize that Jesus paid a great price for our redemption and that *we belong to Him*? The notion of being completely under the authority of and answerable to someone else goes counter to our society's worship of self-reliance

---

[13] I Corinthians 6:19-20
[14] Romans 12:1, 2
[15] Pentecost, Dwight. *Design for Discipleship*. Grand Rapids: Zondervan Publishing House, 1975, pp. 13-21.

and self-promotion (need I even mention the culture of "selfies" posted on social media?).

So, are we prepared to live as His doulos?
What does that mean to you and me in practical terms, today?

Authority

In addition to being a direct message from the risen Christ and the only text identified as being specifically for believers, this portion of Scripture was recognized *at the time of writing* as a treatise to be preserved for posterity. It carries great authority, for John refers to it as "the word of God" and "the testimony of Jesus Christ." In using these terms, John claims divine authority and inspiration for the message.

Similarly, the Old Testament prophets claimed to have received their messages from God, and so these words are reminiscent of the Old Testament phrase, "Thus says the Lord." Remembering the warnings to those in the Old Testament who did not heed the prophets' words, we should be very careful to give considerable attention to this "testimony of Jesus Christ." We dare not ignore it!

Are we even listening?

A Warning!

In conjunction with the seriousness of the message is a warning with regard to tampering with the text. This warning is not in the introduction, but considering the seriousness of it, we should pause and contemplate it:

> For I testify to everyone who hears the words of the prophecy of this book: If anyone adds to these

things, God will add to him the plagues that are written in this book; and if anyone takes away from the words of the book of this prophecy, God shall take away his part from the Book of Life, from the holy city, and *from* the things which are written in this book.[16]

This is serious business. It has overtones of, "In the day you eat thereof . . . " Let us seek to be diligent to listen for and respond to all, nothing more and nothing less, that the Holy Spirit wants for us to receive, as we explore the first portion of the message: John's Patmos encounter with the Alpha and the Omega.

The Promise

In contrast to this serious warning is another unique element of the opening passage: its promise of blessing in verse 3: "Blessed is he who reads and those who hear the words of this prophecy, and keep what is written in it; for the time is near."

We hear today many promises that are overstated at best and fraudulent in many cases – ads that promise everything from renewed youth, with pictures of beautiful girls in their 20s showing how their "wrinkles" have faded with the use of one or another cosmetic miracles (usually illustrated with fair to good jobs of using Photoshop) to losing weight by eating whole grain cereals (no mention of exercise or other measures needed) or taking a magic pill, to saving money on any number of overpriced goods (doesn't a $10,000 discount on a car make you wonder just how much mark-up really is in an

> *. . . the fulfillment of that promise of blessing is as sure as the character of the One who made the promise.*

---

[16] Revelation 22:18, 19, emphasis mine

automobile?). As a result, we tend to ignore promises, taking for granted that we can't trust someone's word or at least we should be extremely cautious.

That cynicism or caution may be wise in many cases, but the One making the promise in Revelation is God Himself, and the fulfillment of that promise of blessing is as sure as the character of the One who made the promise. What that blessing will be is not defined, and likely it will be different for each of us—but if God has promised a blessing, we are infinitely derelict in our responsibilities as disciples to ignore it.

Let us, then, trust that this look at a portion of Revelation will, as promised, bring us a blessing or blessings untold.

Embedded Letters

Another unique feature is the inclusion of seven letters, a distinctively different genre. They are embedded in the text between John's account of his experience on the island of Patmos

and the Revelation he received after looking and seeing a door standing open in heaven. He responded to a voice like the sound of a trumpet that said to him, "Come up here, and I will show you things which must take place after this."[17] John then found himself immediately in the presence of a throne and One sitting on the throne. The content of the seven letters, as well as the revelation that follows are for another study.

We will devote ourselves here, as noted previously, to the events that took place here on earth in John's experience on that Lord's Day.

---

[17] Revelation 4:1

Shall we, together, begin to explore the vision ... venturing into new realms of understanding and spiritual enlightenment as we look at the experience John had with the Lord Jesus Christ, who left heaven to give a personal message to His Church, with accompanying blessings and warnings.

JOHN'S SALUTATION

John's Greeting
John's Doxology
Prophecy

John, to the seven churches which are in Asia: Grace to you and peace from Him who is and who was and who is to come, and from the seven Spirits who are before His throne, and from Jesus Christ, the faithful witness, the firstborn of the dead, and ruler of the kings of the earth. To Him who loved us and washed us from our sins in His own blood, and has made us kings and priests to His God and Father, to Him be glory and dominion forever and ever. Amen. Behold, He is coming with clouds, and every eye will see Him, even they who pierced Him. And all the tribes of the earth will mourn because of Him. Even so, Amen. "I am the Alpha and the Omega, the Beginning and the End," says the Lord, "who is and who was and who is to come, the Almighty."
(Revelation 1:4-8)

CHAPTER TWO

John's Greeting

John, to the seven churches which are in Asia: Grace to you and peace...

John opens his account with a customary formula found often in the New Testament epistles—identification of the recipients and an invocation of divine blessings of grace and peace. The order is important: grace precedes peace. Only when we have experienced God's grace, whereby He draws us to Himself, are we able to know the "peace that passes understanding."[1] Hence, we will look at both terms and what they mean to us personally

Grace

Grace (Gr., *charis*) is an interesting word – it means, simply, God's unmerited favor and kindness that keeps, strengthens, and benefits one. For some of us, that concept was foreign when it was presented to us – we were taught to earn everything, to measure up, to be the "best." It was a "Wow!" moment – God gives his favor based on who *He* is and not on *my* performance?! M__ describes his experience this way:

> *I grew up in an age of achievement, of pressure to be "THE Best." I was not allowed to be merely "the best I could be – no, I had to be "<u>the</u> very best." If I didn't have all "A"s on my report card, I was in big trouble. A report card with less than all "A"s was an indication of a flaw, a failure, a blight. All that my parents could see was the "minus" following the "A." Heaven forbid if I dropped to the level of performing at only a B (for "bad") level!*

---

[1] Philippians 4:7

M___ is not alone. Many people had – perhaps still have – this pressure. So, hearing and receiving the message of *grace* – that God loves us in spite of our frailties and flaws and mistakes and even sins (and we all have them!) – was an overwhelming experience saturated with gratitude and relief. What an amazing truth to embrace – that there is *nothing* we can do to earn God's love – nothing! Further, there is nothing that we can do or fail to do that diminishes it. We are "accepted in the Beloved" because of Jesus Christ.

> *The everyone-gets-a-trophy policy also fails to accept the fact that not everyone is the best at everything – and thereby fails to prepare young people for the realities of life.*

Unfortunately, much of our culture has gone to the other extreme, so that the term "entitled" better defines the attitudes of many people – a counter to the "achievement" culture, but every bit as misguided. In the "entitlement" culture, everyone on the team gets a trophy, regardless of performance or skill or talent – or lack thereof. The psychological reason is that we don't want to hurt anyone's feelings or have anyone feel inferior. Yet rewarding everyone *equally* cheapens the talents and efforts of those who *do* want to excel, and often they are the actual "losers" – and frequently, they give up, for they reason, "What difference does it make to put forth my best effort if everyone gets the same reward?" The everyone-gets-a-trophy policy also fails to accept the fact that not everyone is the best at everything – and thereby fails to prepare young people for the realities of life. This attitude has permeated many portions of society, such that we often don't recognize it.

One person shared the following:

> *I was in a meeting one day with professionals who were assessing their program, and one of the concerns was how to encourage the recipients of financial awards for*

proposed projects (all of whom had advanced degrees) to be more productive. As we went about making comments to topics posted on large sheets of paper spread across several tables, I was surprised to see that one topic addressed what to do about the recipients who had received large sums of "start-up" funds but had not finished their proposed projects and had nothing to report. Being new to this organization, I hesitated to question the process but finally asked about the accountability expected in the process of awarding the funds (e.g., "Did they submit periodic progress reports?"). Apparently, this was a new concept because my colleagues' faces went blank.

At a subsequent meeting, the leader announced that for the next year, the recipients of the awards would have the opportunity to present their "progress" (I noted that the word "accountability" was not used) at four workshops, only two of which they were required to attend. That would give us, *the senior advisors (or something), opportunities to "help" them if they weren't doing what they had proposed to do. I felt like I was being called upon to do my children's homework – and these folks were in professional positions.*

These colleagues all are well-established experts in their fields, and I doubt seriously that they received the coddling (that was my perception of this process) they were proposing for this next generation. Most of the members of the board are younger than I, and so perhaps they were years away from our culture, which expected us to do what we had proposed or explain what circumstances might have prevented our reaching our goals, but we definitely were expected to do our own work. I am certainly not opposed to mentoring; indeed, I'm a great proponent of sharing expertise and providing encouragement, but for us to permit individuals who are in a demanding profession to be allowed to receive funds and then fail to give any explanation for not doing the proposed work (at best) or simply squander them (at worst) is not only irresponsible on all accounts but actually detrimental in the long-run to these individuals' careers and sense of responsibility. The ethics of such is another matter altogether.

When this "entitlement" philosophy transfers to a spiritual level, people think that God's blessings are deserved rather than a matter of grace. Such is a teaching, or at least an attitude, even in some churches today. Further, according to some of the messages attracting thousands on Sunday morning, those supposed blessings are attached to the *world's* concept of what constitutes blessings: no problems (rather than faith and trust when life goes awry – and it does!); wealth or prosperity (rather than "you cannot serve God and mammon"[2]); position and/or popularity (rather than "have this mind in you which was also in Christ Jesus, who humbled himself..."[3]). The list goes on, with a false presentation of the Gospel (Jesus said, "Take up your cross and follow Me!"[4]) undergirded by an evil[5] emphasis on material and temporal attainments. That message not only is false but also diminishes the value of blessing, "for where your treasure is, there will your heart be also."[6] Hence, the attitude toward grace (God's *unmerited* favor) is diminished, at least until we come to recognize the truth of our condition before God – "for all have sinned and fallen short of the glory of God."

---

[2] Matthew 6:24
[3] Philippians 2:5-8
[4] Mark 10:21; Matthew 16:24; Luke 9:23
[5] Note the serpent's temptations in the Garden: wealth, power, position; lust of the flesh, lust of the eyes, pride of life (I John 2:16).
[6] Matthew 6:21

So, before we can proceed, we have to ask if we've responded to the grace of God in Christ Jesus and received the salvation that He, and He alone, provides and offers, free of works. If you have not received that gift from God, you may do so now, by simply acknowledging your sin, your need for salvation, and your trust in the provision of the Lord Jesus Christ, who shed His blood that *you* might be redeemed. (A short prayer is included at the end of this chapter, which you might like to pray – or one similar to it – before you proceed).

Peace

Peace follows grace. Practically, true peace, that which comes when one is reconciled to God, cannot precede grace, for only as one responds to the grace of God in salvation ("for by *grace* are ye saved through faith,")[7] is peace with God made operational, resulting in one being free of condemnation.[8] When we *do* encounter the reality that our lives are not what they should be, that we are not what we would like to be, that life must hold more for us than material possessions, that the source of our unfulfilled potential is sin, that sin separates us from God, and that God in *grace* has made the provision in the cross of Christ to bring us to Himself, and we respond in faith to His offer of salvation in the finished work of Jesus Christ ("It is finished!" He cried from the cross) – then, and only then, can we know the true meaning of "peace." We have, as Paul put it, "peace with God through our Lord Jesus Christ."[9] We experience Jesus' promise of peace, which only He can give.[10] The words to the hymn become ours:

> *Practically, true peace, that which comes when one is reconciled to God, cannot precede grace . . .*

---

[7] Ephesians 2:8
[8] Romans 8:1
[9] Romans 5:1
[10] John 14:27

> Whatever my lot, thou has taught me to say,
> 'it is well, it is well with my soul.'[11]

Do our problems suddenly disappear? Of course not, although many people do testify to experiencing immediate release from bondage to various spiritual, physical, and emotional strongholds. What does happen is that we begin a journey of faith with Christ Jesus. We begin to learn to define and deal with problems from a divine perspective. We begin to realize that the One who died for us also wants us to turn to Him to lead us according to *His* purposes and *His* plans. When we acknowledge that He is in control, regardless of the circumstances, we experience His peace, "which passes understanding,"[12] and we learn to be obedient to the admonition to "give thanks in all things, for this is the will of Christ Jesus in you."[13]

Grace and peace . . .
It is to those who know this grace and peace that the message of Jesus' Revelation is sent.

***Shall we open our hearts and minds to what
the risen Lord has for US?***

Prayer

If you do not know Christ, you can receive this grace and peace by praying a prayer something like this:

Lord Jesus, I have realized that I am a sinner and need to be redeemed. I confess I can do nothing for myself, but I thank you that you have shed your blood on my behalf. I repent – turn from my way of life and to You as my Savior. I receive You, Lord Jesus, and thank You that You have promised to receive all who come to you by faith. I now declare that I belong to You, and I am no longer my own. Praise and thank You!

---

[11] Spafford, Horatio. "It is Well with My Soul."
[12] Philippians 4:7
[13] I Thessalonians 5:18

CHAPTER THREE

John's Doxology

from Him who is and who was and who is to come, and from the seven Spirits who are before His throne, and from Jesus Christ, the faithful witness, the firstborn of the dead, and ruler of the kings of the earth. To Him who loved us and washed us from our sins in His own blood, and has made us kings and priests to His God and Father, to Him be glory and dominion forever and ever. Amen.

John begins with praise for the Triune God – the Father, the Son, the Holy Spirit – in three separate expressions: the one who is and who was and who is to come; the seven Spirits; and the faithful witness, the firstborn of the dead, the ruler of the kings of the earth. These are not idle words – they state three characteristics about our Lord, and they state great truths for those of us who know Jesus Christ.

The Father – *I Am*

As with so much of Revelation, a single phrase is loaded with information, and we do well to recognize the implications of each aspect, although we will look more fully at those related to Jesus Christ.

Eternal Existence

Here, we see in the phrase *from Him who is and who was and who is to come* an expansion of the great *I AM*. God always has been and always will be. God IS. This attribute was spoken to Moses when God sent him to tell the sons of Israel that he had been sent to free them from bondage. When Moses hesitated, wondering how he could possibly have any influence, God's response was for Moses to tell the children of Israel, "I AM has sent me to you."[1] From the Hebrew language, we get the transliteration for God's name, *YHWH*, four letters that are translated *Yahweh*.

Omnipotence

I AM also speaks of God's self-existent pmnipotence, as well as His omniscience: it encompasses the fact that God is the only Supreme Being,[2] having neither beginning nor ending,[3] the Creator of all things.[4] He is all-powerful and all-knowing. Nothing is hidden from His sight, and nothing is beyond His power. It is a *warning* for those who would think they can fool or disobey Him[5]; the Psalmist put it this way:

> Why do the nations rage,
> And the people plot a vain thing?
> The kings of the earth set themselves
> And the rulers take counsel together,
> Against the LORD and against His Anointed, saying,
> "Let us break Their bonds in pieces
> And cast away Their cords from us."
>
> He who sits in the heaven shall laugh;
> The Lord shall hold them in derision.
> Then He shall speak to them in His wrath,
> And distress them in His deep displeasure.[6]

It is a source of *confidence* for those who, by faith in Jesus Christ, call Him *Father*, knowing that He is aware of every aspect of their being and situations, and they are safe therein[7]:

---

[1] Exodus 3:14 (see Exodus 3:13-15)
[2] Isaiah 43:10; 44:6, 8; 45:21, 21; 46:9
[3] Psalm 90:2
[4] Isaiah 44:24
[5] For example, Galatians 6:7, Romans 2:6, I Corinthians 6:9
[6] Psalm 2:1-5
[7] For example, Psalm 139, Luke 12:7

> God is our refuge and strength,
> A very present help in trouble.
> Therefore we will not fear,
> Even though the earth be removed,
>
> And though the mountains be carried into the midst of the sea;
> Though its waters roar and be troubled,
> Though the mountains shake with its swelling.
> . . . .
> The Lord of hosts is with us;
> The God of Jacob is our refuge.[8]

It is a source of *encouragement* for those who serve Him, knowing that despite all circumstances, they have been sent by *I AM*[9] and can say with Paul:

> For this reason I also suffer these things; nevertheless I am not ashamed, for I know whom I have believed and am persuaded that He is able to keep what I have committed to Him until that Day.[10]

Love

In all of this is the incomprehensible fact that God is LOVE, and God loves you and me! It is because of His love and His desire that we know Him and are reconciled to Him that He sent His Son to redeem us.[11] The love of God extends beyond our comprehension and nothing, absolutely nothing! can separate us from it. Paul states this truth succinctly to the church at Rome, in these words:

---

[8] Psalm 46:1-3, 7
[9] John 8:58, 20:21
[10] II Timothy 1:12
[11] John 3:16

> For I am persuaded that neither death nor life,
> Nor angels nor principalities, nor powers,
> Nor things present nor things to come,
> Nor height nor depth, nor any other created thing,
> Shall be able to separate us from the love of God
> Which is in Christ Jesus our Lord.[12]

Many people have difficulty accepting that God not only wants to redeem them but that He also *loves* them. Their reluctance to accept His love is fostered by events in their past: things they have done or things that have been done to them. For some, they think that the sins they have committed are so great that God could never forgive them, and the devil can use this lie to great advantage. H___ is one who has suffered from this lie for years; she put it this way:

> *You have no idea all the horrible things I have done. I started having sex when I was 13. When I was 15, I had an abortion. I got into drugs and sex and stealing and stuff you wouldn't even want to know about. My parents got sick of getting me out of trouble. They threw me out of the house and told me they didn't want to see me again, unless I got my [expletive] together. I was glad to get away from them and all their hypocrisy. But I didn't have no place to go. So I started staying with some people who had an apartment. Then J. came along and promised me he could take care of me. I thought he loved me but he just wanted to use me. No one ever loved me. My parents just wanted me to be better and all the other people cheat and use you. Why would I believe that God cares? Besides, God wouldn't want someone like me because my life is so [expletive] up.*

---

[12] Romans 8:38-38

H___'s words speak to several false conceptions that keep people from coming to God: she needs to "measure up" to be loved, no one can be trusted, and her past is more than God can handle. All of these assumptions are lies, but they are ones that other people voice in one way or another, even when their lives have not been as painful as H___'s.

The Truth counters these lies. See page 38 for some examples of how we can silence the lies the enemy uses to attack and try to defeat us.

Lie(s)	Truth
"I need to measure up" or "I'm not good enough" to be loved.	No one is "good enough": "all have sinned and come short of the glory of God" (Rom. 3:23). But God has taken care of ALL sin in Jesus Christ: "He who knew no sin became sin on our behalf that we might become the righteousness of God in Him" (II Cor. 5:21). Further, God loves on the basis of His character, not our deeds, and says, "You are precious in My sight" (Is. 43:4).
"No one can be trusted."	Instead of trusting people or circumstances, Jesus says, "Come to Me all you who labor and are heavy laden, and I will give you rest" (Matthew 11:28). He also says that He is the Good Shepherd, and the Good Shepherd looks after His sheep (John 10:11-15).
"What I've done is more than God can handle."	That statement implies that God is rather inept. He can handle any and everything we have done. Jesus paid for it, and His blood washes clean all our sins, so that we become whiter than snow (Isaiah 1:18) and God remembers our sins no more, putting them as far as the East is from the West (Psalm 103:12). Further, Jesus makes clear that "Anyone who comes to me I will not cast out [refuse]" (John 6:37).

So much for the enemy's lies! There are ever so many more that he uses to bombard us. We must reject them and replace them with the truth of God, found in the Scriptures.

We don't know what happened to H___ or many others with similar stories. Some of these things we must leave with God. What we *do* know is that He loves each of us and that His desire is for us to reject the lies and receive the Truth.

The question is: Are *you* in Christ Jesus? Have *you* received Him by faith as your Savior and Lord? If not, then the Scriptures testify that the wrath of God remains on you, for only through Jesus Christ is it appeased.[13]

Or, have you come to faith in God, have acknowledged your sin, repented, asked God to forgive you, and received *by faith* the substitutionary work of Jesus Christ on your behalf?[14] For those who can say "yes" to the latter question and are truly experiencing – day-by-day and realizing more each day – the love of God, the words of the hymn by Frederick M. Lehman (1917) take on special meaning:

> The love of God is greater far
> Than tongue or pen can ever tell;
> It goes beyond the highest star,
> And reaches to the lowest hell . . . .
>
> Could we with ink the ocean fill,
> And were the skies of parchment made,
> Were every stalk on earth a quill,
> And every man a scribe by trade;
> To write the love of God above
> Would drain the ocean dry;
> Nor could the scroll contain the whole,
> Tough stretched from sky to sky.[15]

---

[13] John 3:36, 14:6
[14] Romans 3:23, Luke 13:3b, Matthew 3:2, I John 1:9, Hebrews 2:17; Ephesians 2:8-9
[15] Lehman, Frederick M. "The Love of God." (1917; public domain)

That is how much the Father loves you and me – and, as the last stanza says, even more than we can possibly imagine. And, so because He so loved us, the Father sent the Son.[16]

The Spirit – His Complete Sufficiency

John then says that the aforementioned grace and peace also come from "the seven Spirits who are before His throne." There are two basic ways to interpret the phrase *seven Spirits*, which occurs four times in Revelation.[17] We are not involved in getting into great doctrinal or theological discussions here, so suffice that the two primary ways of seeing this phrase relate to (1) Isaiah's prophecy about the seven-fold ministry of the Holy Spirit[18] or (2) the lampstand with seven lamps mentioned in Zechariah.[19]

Symbolically, it refers to the fullness of the Holy Spirit, "seven" being used as a symbol in Scripture for completeness or wholeness. It has particular symbolic relevance with regard to the lampstand in the tabernacle and in later passages in Revelation. We will look at some of these aspects later.

In the passage in Isaiah noted above (a "Messianic" prophecy, meaning that it is a prophecy concerning the coming Messiah), seven characteristics are attributed to the Spirit: of the Lord (God), of wisdom and understanding, of counsel and might, of knowledge and fear of the Lord. "The Spirit of the Lord" stands alone, whereas the other six attributes are arranged in three groups of two each.

These seven attributes may be summarized as follows, noting that they are poured out in full on the Lord Jesus:

---

[16] John 3:16
[17] Revelation 1:4, 3:1, 4:5, 5:6
[18] Isaiah 11:2
[19] Zechariah 4:1-10; 5:6

"The Spirit of the Lord"

This phrase clearly refers to the Third Person of the Godhead, the Holy Spirit, who is equal with the Father and the Son, far from being merely a "force." This phrase in Isaiah specifically relates to the eternal existence of "the Spirit of God [who in creation] was hovering over the face of the waters," [20] who descended upon Jesus at His baptism[21] and subsequently led Him "into the wilderness to be tempted by the devil,"[22] was sent by the Father and the Son,[23] and indwells believers.[24]

The Spirit can be blasphemed against, resisted, insulted, lied to, grieved, and quenched.[25] We do well to familiarize ourselves with these ways in which we may sin against the Spirit, as well as to recognize His attributes and His work in our lives.[26] These include, but are by no means limited to, the Spirit of truth, love, power, self-discipline, love, judgment, and grace.[27]

Before His crucifixion, Jesus promised that he would send another advocate or counselor, who would be with us and in us.

Before His crucifixion, Jesus promised that he would send another advocate or counselor, who would be with us and in us. John Ogilvie, noting that "For many, the Holy Spirit is the least known and understood Person of the Trinity . . .[or] associated almost exclusively with Pentecost the gift of tongues, or the charismatic church . . . [or] is the subject of dispute," says this:

---

[20] Genesis 1:2
[21] Matthew 3:16
[22] Matthew 4:1
[23] John 14:16, 17, 26, 15:26
[24] I Corinthians 3:16
[25] Matthew 12:31, Acts 7:51, Hebrews 10:29, Acts 5:3, Ephesians 4:30, I Thessalonians 5:19, respectively.
[26] A more detailed study of the Holy Spirit (called pneumatology, for *Gr. pneuma* or spirit) is beyond the scope of this book.
[27] John 15:26, 16:13; I John 4:6; II Timothy 1:7; Isaiah 4:4, Zechariah 12:10, respectively.

Above all, we need someone who has the power to heal our painful memories, sharpen our vision of what is best for our future, and catch us up in a purpose beyond ourselves—one that's big enough to fire our imaginations and give ultimate meaning and lasting joy to daily living . . . . He alone has the omniscience, omnipresence, and omnipotence to be the kind of counselor we need. H can help us with our problems, relationships, and decisions for He knows everything. He is with us always, for He never sleeps. He has all power to give us strength and courage, for He is the Holy Spirit with us and wants to live within us.[28]

Have we turned to the Holy Spirit to guide and direct us, or are we among those who know little about Him? Shall we seek to know Him more intimately?

"of wisdom and understanding"

In Hebrew, the term translated "wisdom" refers to supernatural capacity to make correct judgments based on deep spiritual insights, namely God's ability to see all and know all, the end from the beginning. He knows the "plans He has for us, plans for welfare and not calamity" that we might have hope (confidence) in the future.[29] Some people frown on using this Scripture personally today, but I rely on the words of Paul that "All the promises of God in Him are Yes, and in Him Amen, to the glory of God through us."[30] Hence, on many occasions, I have found much solace in this promise, and He has faithfully fulfilled it numerous times. In fact, I will share a personal experience:

---

[28] Ogilvie, Lloyd J. *The Greatest Counselor in the World.* Ann Arbor, Michigan: Servant Publications, 1994, p. 16
[29] Jeremiah 29:11
[30] II Corinthians 1:20

Some years ago, we were going through an exceptionally trying time, with numerous trials, including my father's illness and subsequent death, a hurricane that did excessive damage to people's homes and businesses and destablized the area's economy, a business failure, a child's marriage crumbling, and several other crises, all at the same time. We were stretched very thin, emotionally, psychologically, and spiritually.

Taking a short respite, we wandered into a local Christian book store to browse (maybe we thought just being in the presence of Christian books, being "book-people," would give relief). At any rate, I started meandering through the area that has knick-knacks and other items when I spotted it, hanging high on the wall. There it was: the promise, in huge letters, beautifuly framed, with a 90%-off tag. We quickly got a salesperson who confirmed that the picture, priced at $100 was, indeed, on sale for $10. I told her, "That's for me! It's sold!" We brought it home, and it has hung since that day in the dining room, right off the foyer leading to my study, so that I pass it many times a day. One day a few years later, I sat down to consider what had transpired since that day and was amazed, speechless in fact, at the wonder of all that God had brought to pass in our lives, way too much to mention here, but definitely testimony to the veracity of that promise and its comfort, especially when the future appears dark and foreboding.

Intertwined with wisdom is understanding, the capacity to accept and apply the deeper truths of God's Word, particularly in applying them to decision-making.[31] Just as we can be confident that God will bring good out of bad, we can know that His Spirit will lead us in making wise decisions, when we rely on Him and not our own devices.

---

[31] Note that Proverbs 4:5 gives an intertwining of the two words: "Get wisdom! Get understanding! Do not forget, nor turn away from the words of my mouth."

"of counsel and power"

This term relates to military strategy, which is particularly relevant in spiritual warfare. Today, many people, including Christians, scoff at the concept of angels, demons, spiritual warfare, and the like, but Scripture is full of evidence of all of these. We need to be aware that we are besieged by an enemy who hates all who love Christ. Indeed, Jesus warned us that the enemy comes to "steal, and to kill, and to destroy."[32] Later, Peter cautioned us to "be sober, be vigilant; because your adversary the devil walks about like a roaring lion, seeking whom he may devour."[33] Paul advises us that "our struggle is not against enemies of blood and flesh, but against the rulers, againts the authorities, against the cosmic powers of this present darkness, against the spiritual forces of evil in the heavenly places" and to put on the whole armor of God.[34] A full discussion of the armor is beyond the scope of this book, but we should at least look at some basic principles. In doing so, we will see that each part of the armor ultimately relates to Jesus Christ, which is evidence that part of the Spirit's role is to teach of Him.

> *We need to be aware that we are besieged by an enemy who hates all who love Christ.*

First, we are to fasten the belt of *truth* about our waist – Did Jesus not say, "I am the Way, the *Truth*, and the Life . . . no one comes to the father but by Me"[35]? John testified to such when he wrote. "The Word became flesh and lived among us, and we beheld his glory, the glory of the one begotten Son, full of grace and *truth*."[36] So, basically, *Jesus is our belt*, which we acknowledge by faith.

---

[32] John 10:10
[33] I Peter 5:8
[34] Ephesians 6:10-18
[35] John 14:6
[36] John 1:24

Next, we are to put on the <u>breastplate of *righteousness*</u>. Paul uses the analogy of the Roman soldier's breastplate, which was of grave importance, for it protected an area of extreme vulnerability, his heart, lungs, stomach, liver, and bowels. Our breastplate *is Jesus Christ the righteous One*, and in His death and resurrection, "He was made sin for us that we might be made the *righteousness* of God in Him."

It is through His blood, shed on our behalf, that we can be justified and His righteousness can be imputed to us. So, to "put on" the breastplate means to consciously claim by faith that we have been made righteous and that God is working in us to do His will. Hence, *Jesus is our righteousness.*

> *It is through His blood, shed on our behalf, that we can be justified and His righteousness can be imputed to us.*

We are to have <u>our feet prepared to go out and proclaim the gospel of peace</u>. The spiritual implication is obvious: we must be sure-footed in our faith, through time spent in Scripture, meditation, and prayer. The command does not end with us, however. The *second* aspect is that we are to be ready to go to others and bring peace to their troubled hearts. Romans 5:1 declares that we have peace *with* God through our Lord Jesus Christ. Our peace *with* God is not subjective but objective — a legal fact, if you will. Jesus also gives us the peace *of* God, which is subjective and experiential. We are to proclaim that truth.

Next, we are to take the <u>shield of *faith*</u>, for with faith we are able to quench the flaming arrows of the evil one. The Greek word for shield, *thureos*, conveys the concept of a large shield, one that basically surrounds the individual. *Jesus Christ is that shield*. The psalmist described it this way:

> "For surely, O Lord, you bless the righteous;
> you surround them with your favor as with a shield. (5:12)

Our protection is in our faith, and our victory over the flaming arrows is because our faith is in Jesus Christ and all He has done on our behalf. *He is our shield and protector.*

And, last, we have the sword. All the other parts of the armor had to do with protection. The sword is for waging battle against the enemy. Paul defines that sword as the word of God. Certainly that means *Jesus Christ, the Word become flesh.* It also means the written word. We are to use it against the enemy's onslaught, as we know Jesus did in the wilderness.

All our armor then, is found in Christ Jesus, and our sword is in Him and in the written word. He has provided, and indeed IS, everything we need.

Are we being dutiful in applying the armor by faith – daily?

"of knowledge and fear of the Lord"

This reference relates to knowing God in an intimate way that leads to a deep and abiding reverence. Today, we see little of serious reverence. Although Jesus is our Good Shepherd and calls us friends, He has never ceased to be holy and worthy of reverence. So much of what today is called *praise* is little more than emotional 'rev-up' much akin to the exercise at a football game when cheerleaders lead the people in the stands into shouting cheers. Addressing the emotional, psychological, and physical (neurological) responses that many people mistake for "praise," including the addictive elements, is beyond the scope of this book. However, when we consider later John's response to the risen Christ, we will begin to get a clearer picture of what true adoration is.

The Son – His Reign as Witness, Firstborn, Ruler

When we come to the description of Jesus Christ, we find again that great truths are encapsulated in a few terms, which we will consider individually as they relate to Him, to His reign, and to our relationship with Him.

Faithful Witness

As a witness, one who gives testimony, Jesus Christ was faithful in all ways to reveal the Father, to be obedient to the Father's will, and to demonstrate and fulfill the requirements of the Law. In every temptation, He was faithful to the Father's purposes and rebuked the tempter, using the written Word.[37] In His ministry, He testified that He did only the will of the Father, stating to those who questioned and opposed Him,

> I can of Myself do nothing. As I hear, I judge; and My judgment is righteous, because I do not seek My own will but the will of the Father who sent Me.[38]

In the Garden of Gethsemane, when in anguish for what lay ahead of Him in the redemption of the world, He cried to the Father that He might be spared, but ended with, "nevertheless not My will, but Yours, be done."[39] His submission to the will of the Father is the very antithesis to the enemy's proclamation, "I will ascend into heaven, I will exalt my throne above the stars of God . . . . I will be like the Most High."[40] It shatters the enemy's lie in the Garden that disobedience would lead to "being like god, knowing good and evil."

---

[37] See Matthew 4:1-10 and Matthew 16:23
[38] John 5:30
[39] Luke 22:42
[40] Isaiah 14:13-14. The passage, although relating at one level to the king of Babylon, is considered to give insight into a rebellion that occurred eons ago, when Lucifer (vs. 12) rose up and declared a "five I-will" proclamation of unprecedented pride and arrogance.

The faithfulness of Jesus Christ is for us the guarantee that we can trust Him to be all that He says He will be. His provision and offer of salvation are sure. He is our good Shepherd, and He cares for us, His sheep.[41] He is the Bread of Life,[42] and He feeds us with all the spiritual nourishment that our souls desire and require.[43] He understands and cares for us, and when we cry out, "Lord, help my unbelief!"[44] He comes alongside us and leads us in the way, whatever our journey may involve:

> *Many years ago, I was visiting my ailing grandmother in a "nursing home," more accurately called today "assisted living." She was clearly not pleased with coming to a point in life when her body did not do as she wanted, and she was ready to go home. She didn't want to be around all those "old people"! As we were conversing in a common area, the nurse brought in an "old" woman in a wheel chair and positioned her near us. The woman's mental state was clearly deteriorated, and she was tied into the chair to keep her from falling out. We continued our conversation and then stopped...and listened. From the lips of the mentally and physically deteriorated old lady came a sweet, gentle sound, and we realized she was singing, "I come to the garden alone, while the dew is still on the roses . . . And He walks with me, and He talks with me, and He tells me I am His own, And the joy we share as we tarry there, None other has ever known."*

Whatever her temporal condition, the woman's eternal spirit was rejoicing in the awareness that her Shepherd was with her. He is with us, as well. His promises never fail.

---

[41] John 10:11-27
[42] John 6:32-40
[43] John 4:13, 14; 7:37
[44] Mark 9:24

*We can know we are never alone, because the
Faithful Witness has promised never to leave or forsake us.
Let us claim and proclaim that truth daily.*

Firstborn from the Dead

Jesus was crucified. He was dead. He was buried. These are historical facts. The crucifixion was a horrible, brutal death, a form of Roman punishment reserved for the worst of criminals. Jesus died on a Roman cross, and to make sure He was dead and to speed up the process, one of the Roman soldiers drove a sword into His side.[45] His body was removed from the cross and placed in a tomb. All of these events are recorded in the Gospel accounts. John, who witnessed these events, does not mention them here, however. Instead, he calls Jesus Christ the "firstborn from the dead."

In Judaism, the "firstborn" carried with it certain privileges, namely the chief rights in the inheritance, so it takes on new relevance with regard to having first place in the inheritance of God's kingdom and, thereby, sovereign reign. Certainly, that concept informs what John is saying, but there is much more.

Christianity is not about a dead or dying man on a cross, despite the great work that occurred there, because if that were where the story ends, we would have no hope and we would be, as Paul said, of all men most pitiable:

> But if there is no resurrection of the dead, then Christ is not risen. And if Christ is not risen, then our preaching is empty and your faith is also empty. Yes, and we are found false witnesses of God, because we have testified of God that He raised up Christ, whom He did not raise up—if in fact the dead do not rise. For if the dead do not

---

[45] John 19:34

> rise, then Christ is not risen. And *if Christ is not risen, your faith is futile; you are still in your sins!* Then also those who have fallen asleep in Christ have perished. If *in this life only we have hope in Christ, we are of all men the most pitiable.*[46]

No, the validation of the power of the cross, of the shed blood for our sins, and of Jesus Christ being the propitiation for our sins is the Resurrection:

> But now Christ is risen from the dead, and has become the firstfruits of those who have fallen asleep. For since by man came death, by Man also came the resurrection of the dead. For as in Adam all die, even so in Christ all shall be made alive.[47]

As believers, we have inherited great riches through Jesus Christ. The great cry of victory in the Christian faith is the Resurrection!

Jesus is *not* on the cross! Jesus is *not* dead! He has risen from the dead! He is alive forevermore! Death is conquered! Death no longer has dominion over Him or over us . . . and He is the *firstborn*: we follow Him in death and resurrection.[48]

> *We are joint heirs with Christ, and we will be raised in the last day and shall share in His glory.*[49]

Ruler of the Kings of the Earth

Regardless of what anyone may think or what circumstances may suggest, Jesus Christ has *all* authority. However mighty or powerful someone may be, Jesus is ever so much more so, even as the builder is greater than the building. Any authority or power

---

[46] I Corinthians 15:13-19; italics added
[47] I Corinthians 15:20-22
[48] Romans 6:5, Colossians 2:12
[49] Romans 8:17

that any leader on earth may have comes, ultimately, from the "ruler of the kings of the earth."

In addition to this proclamation by John, we have the words of our Lord Himself. After His Resurrection, Jesus sent His disciples forth with the commission to proclaim the Gospel, telling them boldly, "All authority has been given to Me in Heaven and on earth."[50]

> *Any authority or power that any leader on earth may have comes, ultimately, from the "ruler of the kings of the earth."*

His disciples recognized and proclaimed the Lord's authority as they went forth in obedience to His command. In presenting the good news of salvation to Cornelius' household, Peter proclaimed that Jesus Christ is "Lord of all."[51] In his prayer for the church in Ephesus, Paul declared the

> exceeding greatness of His power toward us who believe, according to the working of His mighty power which he worked in Christ when He raised him from the dead and *seated Him at His right hand in the heavenly places*, far above all principality and power and might and dominion, and every name that is named, not only in this age but also in the age to come.[52]

To the church in Philippi, Paul described the submission and humility of Christ in His incarnation, and then proclaimed the fact that now

> God has highly exalted Him and given Him the name which is above every name, that at the name of Jesus ever knee should bow, of those in heaven, and of those on earth, and of those under the earth,

---

[50] Matthew 28:18
[51] Acts 11:36 (full account, Acts 11:24-48)
[52] Ephesians 1:19-21; italics added

and that every tongue should confess that Jesus Christ is Lord, to the glory of God the Father.[53]

The day is coming when everyone will kneel and acknowledge the supreme authority of the "ruler of the kings of the earth." Those who belong to Him will be exalted with Him; those who do not belong to Him will, nonetheless, acknowledge their great deception and rebellion in refusing to kneel and acknowledge His lordship before it was too late.

Have we acknowledged His lordship in our lives?

His People – Three Truths Concerning Them

In this great doxology, John continues to say that the Faithful One, the Firstborn from the dead, the Ruler of the kings of the earth, extends to His people love, freedom from sin, and position. The order is one of chronological progression, beginning with Christ's love, which existed prior to any response to it ("but God demonstrates His own love toward us in that while we were yet sinners, Christ died for us"[54]); it continues as Christ makes the provision for salvation[55]; and it results in the priesthood of each believer.[56]

How important it is to begin to understand the implications of these provisions. They have great relevance for us as we journey through this transitory life.

---

[53] Philippians 2:9-11
[54] Romans 5:8
[55] II Peter 1:18-21
[56] I Peter 2:9

Loved by Christ

First, Jesus Christ loves us – *you* and *me*! Christianity is not a *religion* – a system of rules and regulations – rather, it is a *relationship* with the living and risen Christ. It is a relationship that begins with God taking the initiative, rather than man trying to find God.[57] This distinction sets Christianity apart from any world or religious system. The relationship begins with love – Jesus loves us – unconditionally! His love is not based on our performance, as noted previously, but on His character. His love continues all our days. Nothing can diminish His love, nothing can override His love, nothing can separated us from His love, which is manifest in the cross:

> *Christianity is not a religion – a system of rules and regulations – rather, it is a relationship with the living and risen Christ.*

> As the Father loved Me, I also have loved you; abide in My love. If you keep My commandments, you will abide in my love . . . This is My commandment, that you love one another as I have loved you. Greater love has no one than this, than to lay down one's life for his friends. You are My friends if you do whatever I command you."[58]

Just stop for a minute and contemplate what Jesus Christ said: He loves *you* as much as the Father loves Him! How much did the Father love Him? Beyond all comprehension, for all eternity. Jesus loves *you* that much!

For many people, the emotional and psychological scars caused by events and people in their lives are so deeply ingrained that they have great difficulty thinking anyone could love them. We are reminded again of M___, who received praise only when he

---

[57] John 3:16
[58] John 15:9-14

accomplished something – and was berated when he fell short of perfection. We also think of H___, who thought that God could not possibly love her because of the sins in her life. Their concepts of "love" were greatly warped, and it was very difficult for them to realize that the Lord Jesus loves them just the way they are, flaws and all. But that's the distinct message of the Scripture; that's the incomprehensible message of the Gospel: Jesus loves *you*. Jesus loves *me*. Period. His love reaches beyond the barriers of self-induced shame, it shatters the facades of self-importance, it heals the pain of rejection, it smashes the strongholds of guilt and anger. It extends beyond our capacity to grasp, and it is offered to all who will receive it, through faith in Jesus Christ.

Another great hymn of the faith by Charles Wesley puts some of these astounding truths into words of praise:

> Amazing love! How can it be,
> That Thou, my God, shouldst die for me?
> . . . .
> He left His Father's throne above
> So free, so infinite His grace —
> Emptied Himself of all but love
> And bled for Adam's helpless race:
> 'Tis mercy all, immense and free,
> For O my God, *it found out me*!
> . . . .
> My chains fell off, my heart was free,
> I rose, went forth, and followed Thee. [59]

This is the love that Jesus Christ extends to you and me. We receive it by faith, and the Holy Spirit works in our hearts to make it become a comfort and a confidence.

We do well to stop and meditate on this truth – often!

---

[59] Wesley, Charles. "Amazing Love." *Psalms and Hymns*, 1738; italics added

Washed in His blood

Second, He has "washed us from our sins in His own blood," and thereby God brings us into fellowship with Himself. Because we all were separated from God by our sin[60] and could do nothing about it ourselves, God made the provision to bridge that gulf.[61]

People don't like to use the word "sin" today – it makes us uncomfortable (isn't that the idea?) if we are told we are sinners. Many preachers today even refuse to mention the word in sermons because they don't want to offend people – they prefer, I suppose, to leave people in their self-deception and lost condition rather than risk their own popularity by presenting truth. God calls them "false shepherds."

What more glorious message is there to give than that the "Good Shepherd," Jesus Christ, has considered our lost condition and has taken care of our sin, which we know we have whether we want to make ourselves uncomfortable or not by using the word! What misguided concept of ministry leads people to withhold the message that Jesus loves you so much that He wants to take care of what separates you from God and bring you into fellowship with Him?

How does He do that? He offers forgiveness and reconciliation with God to those who repent of their sin and receive salvation from Him by faith, based on His shed blood on the cross.[62] Hence, John says to those of us who have come to grips with the reality of our sin and our need for salvation and who have turned to Christ in faith that we have been set free from the bondage of sin, having

---

[60] Romans 3:23
[61] Ephesians 2:8, 9; Titus 3:5
[62] Colossians 1:20

been washed by His blood. This sacrifice was necessary, for "without shedding of blood is no remission"[63] for sin.

> *Having removed the chasm that separated us from God, Jesus Christ invites us into fellowship with Himself.*

All our sins were placed on Jesus Christ on the cross, where the payment for them was made. God remembers our sins no more[64] – the term for "remember" means "to act in accordance with." God no longer acts in accordance with our sins, but in accordance with the shed blood of His Son. What a glorious truth! Our sins bring condemnation, but God no longer acts in accordance with them – we are not condemned; rather, we are cleansed by the blood of Christ and the righteousness of Jesus Christ is credited to us.[65]

Having removed the chasm that separated us from God, Jesus Christ invites us into fellowship with Himself.[66] Rather than being at enmity with God, we have a new relationship, whereby we call him "Abba, Father."[67] This is why John could say,

> That which we have seen and heard we declare to you, that you also may have fellowship with us, and truly *our fellowship is with the Father and with His Son Jesus Christ*.[68]

What an astounding truth: we have fellowship with the Creator of the universe. How does that change how we perceive the world? How we treat other people? How we worship?

---

[63] Hebrews 9:22
[64] Isaiah 4:25, Jeremiah 31:34, Hebrews 8:12
[65] II Corinthians 5:21
[66] I Corinthians 1:9; II Corinthians 13:14; I John 1:7, 2:3-6
[67] Romans 8:15; "Abba Father" has the connotation of endearment, affection, and dependency. The one term is a Syriac word in use by the Jews, and the other a Greek word; it expresses the complete confidence and marks a vehemence of affection and liberty; it is the term Jesus used in prayers (e.g., Mark 14:36).
[68] I John 1:3; italics added

Made His Priests

Third, as if that were not enough – to be loved by Jesus Christ, to be washed in His blood – there is more: when we come to Christ for salvation, He makes us priests in His kingdom to serve his God and Father. This is what is meant by the term, *priesthood of the believer*. In the Hebrew faith, only priests could enter the holy place to bring sacrifices for sins, and only the High Priest could enter the most holy place, once a year on the Day of Atonement, where he made sacrifices for himself and for the nation. The epistle to the Hebrews in the New Testament explains how Jesus Christ is *our* High Priest and that He has made a one-time sacrifice in His own body, once for all.[69] When He died, the veil of the temple, which had separated the people from the presence of God, was rent (or torn) from top to bottom,[70] thereby opening the way for all to come to God through faith in Christ, based on His shed blood.

> *What the High Priest approached with hesitation, even fear, we – redeemed men and women, young and old, rich and poor – now are bid to approach with confidence and boldness.*

In using the term *priests to His God and Father*, John confirms that we have direct access to God the Father, and the writer to the Hebrews says that we are even instructed to come *boldly* not merely to the earth-bound Holy of Holies but to the throne of God's *grace* to receive mercy in time of need.[71] What the High Priest approached with hesitation, even fear, we – redeemed men and women, young and old, rich and poor – now are bid to approach with confidence and boldness. We need not be shy or hesitant. We need not hold back. Christ Jesus beckons us to

---

[69] Hebrews 7:27; 9:12, 26
[70] Matthew 27:51; Mark 15:38
[71] Hebrews 4:16

come, as His redeemed priests, and exercise our prerogatives, made possible by His blood. This is what the last stanza of Wesley's hymn, quoted above, means:

> No condemnation now I dread;
> Jesus, and all in Him, is mine;
> Alive in Him, my living Head,
> And clothed in righteousness divine,
> Bold I approach the eternal throne,
> And claim the crown, through Christ my own.

To this Christ, John attributes all glory and dominion as he turns the focus to the second Advent, when Christ will be "coming with the clouds and every eye will see Him." He is the Alpha and the Omega, and, yes, one day He *is* coming again.

In the meantime, we are called to live into the relationship He has purchased for us.

CHAPTER FOUR

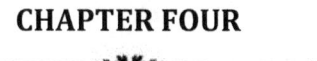

He is Coming!

Behold, He is coming with clouds, and every eye will see Him, even they who pierced Him. And all the tribes of the earth will mourn because of Him. Even so, Amen. "I am the Alpha and the Omega, the Beginning and the End," says the Lord, "who is and who was and who is to come, the Almighty."

One of the great characteristics of this text that we will consider more thoroughly later is the rhetorical element. Here, we note only that John uses the present tense in describing Jesus Christ as the faithful witness, firstborn from the dead, and ruler over kings of the earth; then he uses the past tense for describing what Jesus has done on our behalf so that we might come into relationship with Him and the Father and the Holy Spirit. Now, before proceeding with his story, John makes a prophecy – a statement about the future – concerning our Lord Jesus Christ.

Coming with Clouds

John tells us that, "Behold, He is coming with clouds." This statement clearly echoes Daniel's prophecy:

> I was watching in the night visions,
> And behold, One like the Son of Man,
> Coming with the clouds of heaven!
> He came to the Ancient of Days,
> And they brought Him near before Him.[1]

It also reiterates an earlier statement made by Luke to describe when the resurrected Christ left earth and was "taken up, and a cloud received Him out of their sight" as the disciples watched in

---

[1] Daniel 7:13

wonder. While they were watching – looking steadfastly toward heaven as He went up –

> behold, two men stood by them in white apparel, who also said, "men of Galilee, why do you stand gazing up into heaven? This same Jesus, who was taken up from you into heaven, will so come in like manner as you saw Him go into heaven." [2]

As surely as Jesus Christ came that first Christmas morn, He will come again. Such is the promise of Scripture. In many liturgical churches, this truth is pronounced each Sunday:

> Christ has died,
> Christ is risen,
> Christ will come again.

Past...*died*; present...*risen*; future...*will come again*.

> *If we truly believe [that Christ will come again], certainly our lives should give some evidence of it.*

If we truly believe the third statement, certainly our lives should give some evidence of it. Dr. Dwight Pentecost drew a stunningly beautiful analogy between the relationship we have with our Lord and the betrothal period and marriage in the Jewish culture of Jesus' day. I cannot begin to give justice to his explanation, but suffice that he pointed out how the bride, betrothed to her future husband, awaited his return while he went to prepare a place for her – in everything she said and everything she did, she gave witness to that betrothal and to her love and commitment to her future husband.

---

[2] Acts 1:9

In like manner, our Bridegroom has gone to prepare a place for us and will come again; He will receive us to Himself.³ While He is away, we are His representatives here on earth, and all our actions and words and attitudes give witness to just how much we truly believe that "Christ will come again."

Jesus Christ left one hallmark that would distinguish us as His disciples, His Bride:

> "…Where I am going, you cannot come' so now I say to you. A new commandment I give to you, that you love one another; as I have loved you, that you also love one another. By *this* all will know that you are My disciples, *if you have love for one another*."⁴

> *If our love for one another is the one distinguishing characteristic that we are His disciples, how well are we doing?*

I wonder to what extent we are giving evidence that we belong to Him. If our love for one another is the one distinguishing characteristic that we are His disciples, how well are we doing? If we are to love one another *as He loves us*, how well are we doing?

My friend, Father Link Hullar, puts it this way:

> Love is the priority established by our Lord and Savior Jesus Christ. It is appropriate that we begin with what Jesus said was most important. When asked about His priorities, Jesus replied, "you shall love the Lord your God with all your heart, with all your soul, with all your mind, and with all your strength. That is the first commandment. And the second, like it, is this: You shall love your neighbor as yourself. There is no other

---
³ John 14:2, 3
⁴ John 13:33b-35 (italics added)

commandment greater than these" (Mark 12:30-31).

We must settle in our minds and in our hearts that we have been given a very clear commandment. We must understand that if we are to follow Jesus, if we are to call ourselves Christians, and if we are to obey Jesus, then our priority will be His priority: to love God and to love others.[5]

Jesus also left us a warning to expect that the world will not receive us kindly:

"If the world hates you, you know that it hated Me before *it hated* you. If you were of the world, the world would love its own. Yet because you are not of the world, but I chose you out of the world, therefore the world hates you. Remember the word that I said to you."[6]

What did He mean by these words except that our lives are to be so distinct from the world around us that they bring conviction of sin; our love for God, our relationship with Jesus Christ, our empowering by the Holy Spirit should be so evident in our lives that anyone looking on will see their own need for Christ's redeeming love. Some people will respond and fling themselves upon Jesus, receiving the salvation He offers. However, that will not always

---

[5] Hullar, Link. *Living it Out: Being Jesus' Disciples.* Spring, TX: Cinnabun Sugar Publishing, 2016, p. 17
[6] John 15:18-20

be the case, any more than it was when He walked on this earth among His own people: sometimes, they will hate us, as they hated Him. Sometimes, it will be the religious leaders, even, as it was with Him. So, He warned the disciples, and us, of this fact in advance.

Today, as countless thousands of believers are being forced from their homes, being murdered, and watching their children murdered, even beheaded, we are more acutely aware of the cost of being faithful to Christ. Christianity is not a "prosperity gospel"; it is a radical turning from the world and to God, it is choosing to be Jesus' disciple, it is waiting in expectation for the Bridegroom to come take us home! It is realizing that we may be rebuffed, humiliated, disgraced – even by today's "Pharisees." When Jesus returns, he will come with the clouds, John says. This coming is counter to the first advent, when He

> made Himself of no reputation, taking the form of a bondservant, and coming in the likeness of men. And being found in appearance as a man, He humbled Himself and became obedient to the point of death, even the death of the cross.[7]

Instead of being a helpless, dependent infant born in an indiscriminant place and put in a manger, Jesus Christ will come the second time in great glory[8] with the clouds. His appearing will demonstrate the authority not seen in the tiny babe, who was, despite all appearances, "God incarnate." I wonder how often, when we sing at Christmas the carol "Hark! The Herald Angels Sing," do we grasp the magnitude of these words:

> Veiled in flesh the Godhead see
> Hail the incarnate Deity
> Pleased as man with man to dwell
> Jesus, our Emmanuel.[9]

---

[7] Philippians 2:7,8
[8] Matthew 16:27; Colossians 3:4
[9] Wesley, Charles. "Hark! The Herald Angels Sing" (1739)

The eternal glory, that glory He had with the Father before the world began,[10] will no longer be veiled by His humanity. The supreme authority will not be laid aside; instead, He will come with power and might.

Every Eye Shall See Him

Everyone, John says, including those "who pierced Him," will be aware of His coming, and Paul wrote that

> we shall all stand before the judgment seat of Christ. For it is written:
> > "As I live, says the Lord,
> > Every knee shall bow to Me,
> > And every tongue shall confess to God."[11]

Furthermore, Paul told the church in Philippi that

> At the name of Jesus every knee should bow, of those in heaven, and of those on earth, and of those under the earth, and that every tongue should confess that Jesus Christ is Lord, to the glory of God the Father.[12]

The time is coming when everyone, everywhere will bow before the Lord of lords; they will confess Him to be Lord, and God the Father will be glorified in that utter submission of all humanity to the One who is the Way, the Truth, the Life, the only One through whom a person may approach the Father. Nowhere are we offered any suggestion that this submission will result in one's salvation; rather, the submission to Jesus Christ and the acknowledgement of His Lordship must come prior to that day for one to be saved, redeemed, born again.

---

[10] John 17:5
[11] Romans 14:10b, 11; Paul quotes from Isaiah 45:23; see also Philippians 2:10-11
[12] Philippians 2:10, 11

We don't know when that day of judgment will come, nor did Paul, which is perhaps one reason he made this point to the church in Corinth:

> We then, as workers together with Him, also plead with you not to receive the grace of God in vain. For He says,
>
>> "In an acceptable time I have heard you.
>> And in the day of salvation I have helped you."
>
> Behold, now is the accepted time; behold, now is the day of salvation.[13]

The writer to the Hebrews, invoking Psalm 95:7-8, issued this call:

> For we have become partakers of Christ if we hold fast the beginning of our confidence steadfast to the end, while it is said:
>
>> "Today, if you will hear His voice,
>> Do not harden your hearts as in the rebellion." . . . .
>
> Since therefore it remains that some must enter it [His rest], and those to whom it was first preached did not enter because of disobedience, again He designates a certain day . . . .
>
>> "Today, if you will hear His voice,
>> Do not harden your hearts."[14]

Is He speaking to you today? Is Jesus calling you to follow Him? Today is the day of salvation.

---

[13] II Corinthians 6:1-2
[14] Hebrews 3:14-15; 4:6-7

All the Tribes Will Mourn

John speaks of a future day, when the truth of who Jesus is will be revealed, and, in addition to bowing before Him and acknowledging that He is Lord of lords and King of kings, everyone who has rejected Him will mourn. John echoes Zechariah's prophecy that

> "I will pour on the house of David and on the inhabitants of Jerusalem the Spirit of grace and supplication; then they will look on Me whom they pierced. Yes, they will mourn for Him as one mourns for his only son, and grieve for Him as one grieves for a firstborn."[15]

Those who deny and reject His offer of salvation are the ones who will, one day, join the throngs of those who mourn, rather than those who sing "hallelujah" because they are recipients of His salvation. They will not only mourn; their part, Jesus Christ said, will be "in the lake that burns with fire and brimstone, which is the second death."[16]

Will you mourn? Or
Will you be among those who receive from Him
the "spring of the water of life without cost"?[17]

The Alpha and Omega

> "I am the Alpha and the Omega . . . who is and who was and who is to come, the Almighty." (Revelation 1:8) "Behold, I make all things new . . . Write, for these words are true and faithful." (Revelation 21:5)

This is the one who is Coming Again!

---

[15] Zechariah 12:10
[16] Revelation 21:8
[17] Revelation 21:6

JOHN'S NARRATIVE

John's "Story"
Day to Be Remembered
Instruction

I, John, both your brother and companion in the tribulation and kingdom and patience of Jesus Christ, was on the island that is called Patmos for the word of God and for the testimony of Jesus Christ. I was in the Spirit on the Lord's Day, and I heard behind me a loud voice, as of a trumpet, saying, "I am the Alpha and the Omega, the First and the Last," and, "What you see, write in a book and send it to the seven churches which are in Asia: to Ephesus, to Smyrna, to Pergamos, to Thyatira, to Sardis, to Philadelphia, and to Laodicea."
(Revelation 1:9-11)

CHAPTER FIVE

John's Story

I, John, both your brother and companion in the tribulation and kingdom and patience of Jesus Christ, was on the island that is called Patmos for the word of God and for the testimony of Jesus Christ.

The story begins! John divides the narrative into three portions: the background concerning his circumstances and the setting, the vision he had of the risen Christ, and the commission Christ gave him. This is an exciting tale, and in each instance John uses symbolism and other rhetorical devices to try to capture the moment in time for future readers. We will look at each of the three sections individually.

The Background

John begins his story by identifying himself, but he does more than merely provide a name: he establishes a bond with the reader, using the term, "your brother." So, this is not a story for just any indiscriminant reader. Rather, it is a story for all the members of the family, God's family – that's *you* and *me*, as well as all the saints who have come before us and will come after us, until Jesus returns.

Family Bond

John speaks of three aspects regarding the family bond. Have you noticed how often he uses a group of three items (called a *triad*)? There is a Trinitarian aspect to his message, from beginning to end. This is one of those characteristics considered a "rhetorical device," and John may have used this triad as a constant reminder of the triune God, as well as an emphasis on the One "who is and who was and who is to come." John says he "shares" these three aspects with them, and with us:

Tribulation

First, we will experience some form of tribulation. The specific tribulation John mentions is, no doubt, the persecution the Christians were experiencing during Domitian's reign. However, tribulations in the context of being a Christian can have deeper and broader implications. Contrary to some of the popular teachings of the "prosperity gospel," which liken God to a cosmic Santa Claus who spreads cheer in the form of material gifts, the call to follow Jesus is costly. Repeatedly in the Gospel accounts, Jesus informs His disciples and others that following Him requires commitment and, sometimes, great cost in this life. As we saw in the previous chapter, our relationship with Him will draw animosity from others, as He explained:

> "If you were of the world, the world would love its own. Yet because you are not of the world, but I chose you out of the world, therefore the world hates you. Remember the word I said to you, 'A servant is not greater than his master.' If they persecuted Me, they will also persecute you. If they kept My word, they will keep yours also. But all these things they will do to you for My name's sake, because they do not know Him who sent Me."[1]

Jesus Christ also warned specifically of tribulation that His disciples were likely to encounter, when He said:

---

[1] John 15:19-21

> "Then they will deliver you up to tribulation and kill you, and you will be hated by all nations for My name's sake."[2]

And again,

> "These things I have spoken to you, that in Me you may have peace. In the world you shall have tribulation; but be of good cheer, I have overcome the world."[3]

The history of Christendom is replete with instances of the tribulation, including death, that Jesus' followers have experienced for their faith. Should anyone question the cost of following Jesus, he or she might simply do a quick study of how each of the disciples died. In the past century, we have the example of Dietrich Bonhoeffer, the German Lutheran pastor and theologian who, even while in prison, continued his fight for the faith, until on April 8, 1945 he was led naked to the execution yard and hanged. In 2015, young school girls were kidnapped from their school by terrorists, because of their Christian faith; at the time of this writing, their fate remains unknown. Worldwide, terrorists are intent upon killing Christians.

Great tribulation? Yes! But, there is the comfort of knowing that even in the midst of that tribulation, Jesus is with us, He will never leave or forsake us,[4] and He provides peace, *His* peace, about which the world knows nothing.[5]

Are we prepared to face criticism and even tribulation for standing for the faith once delivered?

---

[2] Matthew 24:9
[3] John 16:33
[4] Hebrews 13:5
[5] John 14:27

The Kingdom

A *second* aspect of our common bond in Jesus Christ is the Kingdom. We are part of Christ's Kingdom, which is not of this world:

> Jesus answered, "My kingdom is not of this world: if my kingdom were of this world, then would my servants fight, that I should not be delivered to the Jews: but now is my kingdom not from here."

Jesus is King of His kingdom - He calls his subjects - His disciples - to give unwavering submission to His Lordship.

Jesus chose not to take us immediately into heaven with Him but to leave us here with a job to do: to bring in the Kingdom. Jesus Christ told His disciples, in giving the model prayer (sometimes called "The Lord's Prayer), to pray, "thy kingdom come."

The implications are far beyond the scope of this book, but for our purposes, shall we focus on one aspect of a kingdom: there is a King, and that King reigns, and those who are in the kingdom are subjects to the King. Pretty simple stuff - were it so simple to live accordingly! Jesus is King of His kingdom - He calls his subjects - His disciples - to give unwavering submission to His Lordship: He calls the shots, He makes the decisions, He leads the way.

When we live in submission to His Lordship, then, even in tribulation, we have *peace*. Do you see how these aspects of our bond are intertwined?

Another consideration of the kingdom is that we have authority in His name, *now*... and we shall reign with Him in the future, if we endure. This is the hope, or confidence, that we have in our King.

Patience

Third, we need patience. The word translated "patience" is *hupomone*, which carries with it the idea of endurance regarding things or circumstances. Here, again, the text counters the false teaching that the Christian life is to be free of problems, else why would we possibly need endurance – *patient* endurance, at that?

The writer to the Hebrews says that we need "patient endurance" so that we will continue to do God's will, for we are called to live by faith, knowing that in the proper time, Christ *will* come.[6] Endurance is more than merely gritting our teeth and waiting for the ordeal to pass; rather, for Christ's disciples, it has great reward and it means to embrace the moment, to welcome the ordeal, to

> Greatly rejoice, even though now for a little while, if necessary, you have been distressed by various trials, so that the proof of your faith, being more precious than gold which is perishable, even though tested by fire, may be found to result in praise and glory and honor at the revelation of Jesus Christ.[7]

Paul said much the same to the church in Rome:

> And not only this, but we also exult in our tribulations, knowing that tribulation brings about perseverance; and perseverance, proven character; and proven character, hope; and hope does not disappoint, because the love of God has been poured out within our hearts through the Holy Spirit who was given to us.[8]

---

[6] Hebrews 10:36-38
[7] I Peter 1:5-7
[8] Romans 5:4

Setting and Situation

Narratives have settings, as well as characters and events. John's narrative is no exception. He tells us that the events took place on the island of Patmos, to which he had been exiled; the location is not nearly as important as the *reason he was there*. As the narrative opens, John provides some personal information. In narrative theory, we sometimes call this sort of digression an "embedded narrative" because it tells a story within another story – sometimes a very detailed one, and sometimes, as here, a very short one, but one that is packed with implications.

In this very short embedded narrative, John says that he was exiled to this island for his faith, for "the word of God and for the testimony of Jesus Christ." That's an interesting comment. So, what's all this about if we do the right thing, if we pray the right prayer, if we "beeeellllieeeve" just the right way, God will send down showers of blessings and material goods? John's testimony (need I mention Jesus' life, abuse, crucifixion?) is that sometimes (often?) when we are faithful, things do *not* go our way. Teaching to the contrary is not only unbiblical but can be disastrous in individuals' lives. S___ tells of learning this lesson the hard way, after being deceived for years:

> Back in the mid-'70s and early '80s, a certain speaker traveled around the country holding seminars about conflicts in life and how to resolve them, as well as steps to getting God's blessings. The seminars were attended by thousands of evangelical believers, who for many years bought this teaching "hook, line, and sinker." It seemed to be very biblical because the speaker spattered Scripture references, which supposedly supported what he was saying, on the overhead images. People returned year after year, each time taking more notes and adding more material to their red notebooks (handed out the first time they attended).

> *Among the numerous mistaken notions taught in that seminar was one about steps to having godly children, as if they have no free wills. It sounded good, but the problem was, as one pastor friend said, "That's all great, but my son didn't read the red notebook!" Well, of course, at least that portion of the teaching was false, and it put heavy burdens on parents that God, who certainly could understand having rebellious children (did He not have quite a lot of experience with that, despite being a perfect "parent" to Israel?), never intended.*
>
> *The underlying lie was that if we do the right things, life will go our way. Obviously, nothing could be further from the truth: Jesus did everything right, and He ended up on a cross. The prophets and disciples and faithful believers down the ages who were martyred gave their lives for the truth, for doing what was right! So much for the "red notebook" notion regarding rearing perfect children.*

So much, too, for the "prosperity gospel" notion that God intends for His people to be free of adversity and trials and challenges.

John says he had been exiled *for being faithful in presenting the Gospel*. Today, many people are being persecuted in one fashion or another for being faithful to God's Word, for upholding the Creeds, for refusing to succumb to pressure to water-down the Gospel (e.g., no talk about sin, blood of Christ, salvation through Jesus Christ alone) – and I'm talking about within the churches – far worse things are happening around the world to believers who stand firm in their faith to the point of death. Once again, I quote my friend, Fr. Link Hullar, who states it this way:

> Jesus tells His friends about the life and ministry that they are to embrace. He speaks to them and, of course, to us, as well. He communicates a basic truth that needs to register with us at all levels. If

Jesus, the Teacher, is misunderstood (His message distorted, perverted, and corrupted), then how can we expect anything different as we attempt to be His messengers. If Jesus, the Master, is abused (even tortured and executed), then why might we, His servants, expect to be treated any differently? If Jesus is willing to humble Himself in order to wash the feet of His friends and to die a painful, humiliating death upon the cross, then what are our expectations as we follow Him? He wants us to have some realistic concept regarding the costs of discipleship. He wants us to have a reasonable notion of what a life lived as His messenger and servant will mean. If we do NOT understand, then we will face a lifetime of disappointment and confusion. However, IF we can grasp the basic concept of our servant/messenger/ friendship with Jesus, then we can find happiness in that relationship and in His service. If we expect things to turn out much better for us than it did for Him, then we are sadly mistaken; happiness is certain to elude us.[9]

Rather than being surprised or disheartened, we should be joyful, realizing that this is how it is in this age, and that our reward will come at a later time.

---

[9] Hullar, Link. *Becoming Jesus' Disciples: Asking, Searching, Knocking . . .Together.* Cinnabun Sugar Publishing, division of Hulden Publishing, 2014, p. 101.

CHAPTER SIX

A Day to Remember

I was in the Spirit on the Lord's Day, and I heard behind me a loud voice, as of a trumpet, saying, "I am the Alpha and the Omega, the First and the Last . . ."

John's story turns from the past – why he was on the island of Patmos – to the day at hand, the day he received the Revelation from Jesus Christ. What an exciting moment this is! It comes, apparently after John had been on the island for some time, exiled and alone. We don't know what he had experienced there prior to that day. Scripture is silent about those days of exile, but we know that Patmos was used as a penal settlement for people who were considered a threat by the Roman authorities. It must have been a very unpleasant experience, at best. Yet, he remained faithful and went about his customary practice of worship on the Lord's day.

Then, suddenly, with no warning, his day-to-day routine was interrupted! Jesus Christ appeared. The intervention was much like so many other times in Scripture, especially in the Old Testament, when individuals were going about their usual, sometimes mundane, tasks, and God moved in and changed everything. In fact, the entire history of Israel is a pattern of divine interventions into the lives of ordinary people as they went about their ordinary daily lives until the day God interrupted and changed the course of things forever. The New Testament is a continuation of that pattern, or motif. It was certainly Mary's experience, when the angel appeared to her and told her she was about to be pregnant and would give birth to the long-awaited Messiah. When Jesus Christ appeared on the scene and began His public ministry, He did so by calling ordinary men and women to follow Him, never to be the same again.

It is a great lesson for all of us, for so often the directions of our lives are changed unexpectedly while we are going about our daily tasks. Also, we should learn from John's circumstances that what may seem at the moment to be a terrible situation may be the very place God has placed you or me to give us a special insight or to initiate a new ministry. It may be likened to the truth that

> John's banishment gave opportunity to receive the word of God and testimony of Jesus Christ which came to him in Patmos and subsequently to publish it.[1]

Three clauses describes that moment: he was in the Spirit, it was the Lord's Day, he suddenly heard a voice like a trumpet speaking behind him. We will look at them in the order they appear in the text. Later, we will look at a fourth portion of John's "memoire": the commission. Each of these items is worthy of an individual study, but we will approach them only briefly to get a sense of John's experience and how it relates to our own lives and ministries.

In the Spirit

The words *in the Spirit* encompass a multitude of meanings, far beyond our present study. We are not really sure what John meant by the term. It may have been an experience similar to the one Paul describes in II Corinthians 12:2-4:

---

[1] Beasley-Murray, G. R. *The Book of Revelation*. Grand Rapids: Wm. B. Eerdmans Publ. Co., 1981, p. 64.

> I know a man in Christ who fourteen years ago — whether in the body I do not know, or whether out of the body I do not know, God knows — such a one was caught up to the third heaven. And I know such a man — whether in the body or out of the body I do not know, God knows — how he was caught up into Paradise and heard inexpressible words, which it is not lawful for a man to utter.

Even Paul was not absolutely sure, some 14 years later, exactly what he had experienced. What is important is that his glimpse into the third heaven, or the abode of God, gave him a completely different concept of life, such that he knew to be absent from the body is to be present with the Lord.[2] He was able to endure much suffering, realizing that "our light affliction" is "but for a moment . . . working for us a far more exceeding and eternal weight of glory."[3] It gave him the desire to depart this life and be with the Lord, even though he knew he still had things to do here on earth.[4] It certainly eliminated any fear of death! What it did *not* do was cause him to elevate himself.

For John, the term referred to a state or attitude or time of contemplation and worship, for it preceded the vision. This is an important distinction to make to avoid going astray and associating the term with the vision, which came later. Being "in the Spirit" is a spiritual place intended for all believers, for all believers are indwelt by the Spirit, who teaches, guides, comforts, leads, and testifies of the Lord. Jesus Christ was quite clear about this fact when he told the disciples that He was leaving but that He would

> "pray the Father, and He will give you another Helper, that He may abide with you forever – the Spirit of truth, whom the world cannot receive, because it neither sees Him nor knows Him; but

---

[2] II Corinthians 5:8
[3] II Corinthians 4:17
[4] Philippians 1:22-23

you know Him, for He dwells with you and will be in you . . . The Helper, the Holy Spirit, whom the Father will send in My name, He will teach you all things, and bring to your remembrance all things that I said to you."[5]

In addition, after His Resurrection, Jesus explained things pertaining to the kingdom of God for some forty days before assembling the disciples and commanding them not to depart from Jerusalem but to wait for the promised Spirit. He told them that they were not to know the times or the seasons concerning the Kingdom, but added,

"You shall receive power when the Holy Spirit has come upon you; and you shall be witnesses of Me in Jerusalem, and in all Judea and Samaria, and to the end of the earth."[6]

Then He departed and returned to the Father. An interesting correlation to this promise of power to share the Gospel is found in Jesus Christ's remark that, "When the Helper comes, whom I shall send to you from the Father, the Spirit of Truth who proceeds from the Father, *He will testify of Me* "[7] So, the Spirit also guides

"into all truth; for He [does] not speak on His own authority, but whatever He hears He will speak; and He will tell [of] things to come. He *will glorify Me [Jesus Christ],* for He will take of what is Mine and declare it to you."[8]

The evidence of being in the Spirit is not having visions or revelations or other sensational manifestations but living a life characterized by loving others as Christ loved us and by

---

[5] John 14: 16, 17, 26
[6] Acts 1:8
[7] John 15:26; italics added
[8] John 16:13, 14; italics added

demonstrating the fruit of the Spirit. It is seen in what John MacArthur calls a "true measure of a man of God":

> The true measure of a man [or woman] of God does not lie in his claims of visions and experiences with God, or the force of his personality, the size of his ministry, his educational degrees, or any other human criteria. A true man of God is marked by how much he has suffered in the war against the kingdom of darkness, how concerned he is for people, how humble he is, and how accurately he handles the supernatural revelation found in God's Word (II Tim 2:15).[9]

For John, it meant worshipping the Lord Jesus Christ, there on that island. Despite being alone, bereft of friends and colleagues, and living among criminals, he remained faithful to the ever-present One who promised never to leave or forsake him. His focus was on Jesus Christ: he was in the Spirit!

It is the same for us. Being in the Spirit means that our eyes are on Jesus Christ, not ourselves, not our circumstances, not others. I am reminded of the powerful words in this refrain:

> Turn your eyes upon Jesus,
> Look full in His wonderful face,
> And the things of this earth will grow strangely dim,
> In the light of His glory and grace.[10]

Are we in the Spirit? Are we glorifying Jesus Christ?
Are we even seeking to be in the Spirit?

---

[9] Macarthur, John. *The MacArthur New Textament Commentary. 2 Corinthians.* Chicago, IL: Moody Publishers, 2003, p.396
[10] Lemmel, Helen H. (1922) "Turn Your Eyes Upon Jesus." The Cyber Hymnal http://www.hymntime.com/tch/htm/t/u/turnyour.htm

The Lord's Day

The Lord's Day, as Swete argues, is "the day consecrated to the Lord," noting that, according to other writings dated not much later than this text, it would have been the first day of the week, namely the day of the Lord's Resurrection. Much discussion surrounds the Greek term, *kuriakos*, with regard to its use here and in other texts.[11] We are looking, however, at John's personal experience, and what stands out is his faithfulness, in spite of his circumstances. It is the day consecrated – set apart – to the Lord. Regardless of what had occurred previously – how dire his surroundings, how challenging his companions in the penal colony – John kept the day as holy unto the Lord. What a difference his attitude is to those of so many people who think that Sunday is a day for rest or recreation, or that church is intended for their enjoyment and entertainment rather than a holy day set apart for the worship of the Lord. N___ tells of being part of trying to start a small church plant:

> *We had all been in one church together, but then one of the priests left, and we were really upset because the church had lots of problems and she had been the only one who seemed to care about anyone. She also could teach the Bible, and most of us had never been in a Bible study before – we certainly hadn't had any teaching in the church before she came. We kept hoping we could get her to just break away and start her own church, but she said that was not the way things were done. So, most of us just quit going to church at all.*
>
> *Then, lo and behold, she did leave that church and went with another one that was starting new local churches. We were so thrilled when she agreed to come our way and help us launch a new church. And the Lord provided us with so many things. In fact, while other people were having all sorts of trouble finding a place to meet, we soon had a really good deal: another church*

---

[11] Swete

meeting in the area opened their facility to us to use on Sunday mornings because they met on Sunday afternoons. They were so generous it was just unbelievable. We rejoiced in the Lord's provision.

Then, wouldn't you know it. Almost immediately after we began meeting in the new place, S__ started complaining because the place was so big. The next week, she realized we were sitting on chairs (upholstered and padded!) instead of pews, and she was use to pews! It wasn't long before A__ got grumpy about the backdrop, which held the other church's musical instruments – it just didn't look right, and he couldn't worship looking at guitars. Then, the priest wouldn't let D__ tell her how to do everything, and D__ got all in a tizzy and started telling everyone that things just weren't the way she wanted them!

Well, things went on like that for many months, until we had a meeting and decided to move into a time of "greater discernment about our purpose and mission"; we agreed to disband for a while and pray for the next step. I think we all knew, though, that that was it. A couple of the folks went to other churches, but most of them now just enjoy having Sundays off from work.

What a sad commentary and contrast to John's worshipful stance. The difference, of course is found in the words, "I was in the Spirit"; when we look at the two attitudes, we see the difference between being in the Spirit and being in the flesh. The Spirit *worships*, whereas the flesh *complains*; the Spirit *submits*, whereas the flesh *demands*; the Spirit exalts the *Lord Jesus Christ*, whereas the flesh caters to *self*…and the list goes on and on.

I wonder which attitude best characterizes us.
Are we worshipping God in the Spirit,
or are we exercising our fleshly desires to satisfy ourselves?

Voice Like a Trumpet

John heard a voice – one like a trumpet – behind him. The use of the simile ("like a...") of a trumpet has some interesting implications. We must be careful not to put too much emphasis on the trumpet, but we can safely draw some insights from its use in the Old Testament and then again in the New, as it relates to Jesus' second coming.

Old Testament Instances

The trumpet is first associated with the great day when the Lord God came down on Mount Sinai in the sight of all the people. Moses followed the Lord's instructions to consecrate the people, to have them wash their garments, and to set boundaries, telling them not to go up the mountain or touch its border, lest they die. On the third day, there were thunder and lightning flashes and a thick cloud on the mountain, and

> *The sound of the trumpet* was very loud, so that all the people who were in the camp trembled. And Moses brought the people who out of the camp to meet with God, and they stood at the foot of the mountain . . . . when the blast of the trumpet sounded long and became louder and louder, Moses spoke, and God answered him by voice. Then the Lord came down on Mount Sinai, on the top of the mountain. And the Lord called Moses to the top of the mountain, and Moses went up.[12]

Shortly thereafter, Moses was given the Ten Commandments.

Subsequently, God gave Moses instructions for having a feast or memorial of trumpets that was to be a holy convocation; this feast later became Rosh Hashanah, the New Year. Its purpose was to

---

[12] Exodus 19:10-25; italics added. See also Hebrews 12:18-21

present Israel before the Lord for His favor, and it preceded by only a few days the Day of Atonement. They were to make an offering by fire to the Lord,[13] so the trumpet was associated with an annual event of worship and in preparation for the great Day of Atonement (Yom Kippur).

In Numbers 10, God gave instructions for making two trumpets of hammered silver (the others were rams' horns, or shofar) and told him to "use them for calling the congregation and for directing the movement of the camps" (vs. 2). One shrill blast was to be used to call the people to assemble themselves together before the tabernacle of the Lord. The same sound was to be used to call the people together for the march as they continued their journey. The sons of Aaron, the priests, were to blow the trumpets, and "these [were] to be to [them] as an ordinance forever throughout [their] generations." A trumpet was to be sounded before going to war (vs. 9), and finally "in the day of your gladness, in your appointed feasts, and at the beginning of your months, *you shall blow the trumpets* over your burnt offerings and over the sacrifices of your peace offerings; and they shall be a memorial for you before your God: I am the Lord your God" (vs. 10; italics added).

> . . . the trumpet clearly was associated with special events that demonstrated the Jews' special relationship with Yahweh.

We learn from these passages that the trumpet clearly was associated with special events that demonstrated the Jews' special relationship with Yahweh. Further, it was used to gather God's people.

Jesus Christ's Second Advent

Jesus referred to the trumpet's blast at the second coming in words that are almost identical to the ones John used earlier to

---

[13] Leviticus 23:23-25

describe the Lord, as well as those used in the Old Testament for special events and the calling together of the Lord's people:

> "Immediately after the tribulation of those days the sun will be darkened, and the moon will not give its light; the stars will fall from heaven, and the powers of the heavens will be shaken. Then the sign of the Son of Man will appear in heaven, and then all the tribes of the earth will mourn, and they will see the Son of Man coming on the clouds of heaven with power and great glory And He will send His angels with *a great sound of a trumpet*, and they will gather together His elect from the four winds, from one end of heaven to the other."[14]

Paul also makes reference to the trumpet of God that will sound to gather God's people when the "Lord Himself will descend from heaven with a shout, with the voice of an archangel."[15]

> And when He sounds at last *the great trumpet of redemption, the blessed and mighty blast* of which will reach every ransomed ear, He will gather around Him by that sound, the great and glorious company that no man can number, redeemed out of every kindred, and nation, and tongue, at the cost of His precious blood. Then will the great congregation at length be assembled, in the glorious tabernacle not made with hands; and the eternal song of praise be raised to our God, by the Lord Himself, the chief musician; and one vast Hallelujah chorus from heaven and earth will echo the joyful sound.[16]

---

[14] Matthew 24:29-31; italics added
[15] I Thessalonians 4:16; italics added
[16] Soltau, Henry W. *The Tabernacle, The Priesthood, and the Offerings.* Grand Rapids, MI: Kregel Publications 1972, p. 105-106

Consistent in all of these passages is that the trumpet was associated with a special event, calling, and message from God. Certainly the association holds true for the message that John will receive from the "Alpha and the Omega, the First and the Last."

Are we ready to respond to a "trumpet call"?

CHAPTER SEVEN

Instruction

> "What you see, write in a book and send it to the seven churches which are in Asia: to Ephesus, to Smyrna, to Pergamos, to Thyatira, to Sardis, to Philadelphia, and to Laodicea."

Similar to what Moses experienced on Mount Sinai is the instruction that John received. The NKJV includes the words, "I am the Alpha and the Omega, the First and the Last" in the commission given to John. As Moses was given the Law by the great I AM for God's redeemed people, so John was given messages for the (redeemed) Church. John received this instruction twice: first, by the voice he heard behind him and then again by the Lord, after he turned to witness His appearance.

Write It: The Message

An interesting comparison can also be made between the instructions given to John and those given to Daniel much earlier. Here, John was told to write down everything he was about to see and then to distribute the message among seven churches. This instruction is dichotomous to the instruction given to Daniel concerning the vision he had; in that instance, Yahweh told Daniel that

> "the vision of the evenings and the mornings which has been told is true; but *seal up the vision*, for it pertains to many days hence . . . . But you, Daniel, *shut up the words* and *seal the book*, until the time of the end."[1]

---
[1] Daniel 8:26;12:4a; italics added

Both of these events deal with messages about future events. Both messages are from God. What is different is what the individuals are told to do with them.

> *... how God may work in your life is not necessarily how He will work in my life, and, of course, vice versa.*

We can learn an important lesson from this distinction: namely, that God deals with individuals, and He deals with them differently. So, what relevance does this distinction have for us? Basically that how God may work in your life is not necessarily how He will work in my life, and, of course, *vice versa*. Herein lies a matter that often is overlooked, ignored, or just not known when someone uses an account in Scripture to make unwarranted generalizations and extends the application into every situation.

> *I remember many years ago hearing a preacher teaching on the account of Jesus healing an individual. He told that person to go and tell everyone what Jesus had done for him. From that statement, the preacher drew a global conclusion that was probably quite sincere but incredibly misguided: "you go tell what Jesus has done for you! We are to tell everyone what Jesus has done!" Well, that may very well be the case – sometimes! But not always. As I listened to the highly emotional plea, what came to my mind was the admonition, "Tell no man." Jesus gave this instruction, the very opposite of what He had said previously, after raising an individual from the dead.*

"Go and tell." "Tell no man." What's going on here? Is Jesus confused? Not hardly. Is He contradicting Himself? Impossible. So, what conclusion can we draw from these dichotomous instructions? I'm not sure what all may be involved, but this much is certain: Jesus Christ works differently in each of our lives, and He has specific, personal purposes for each of us. Some of us are to "go and tell" and some of us are to "tell no man."

Further, sometimes, we are to share and other times we are to remain silent. When, where, and with whom we share what God has done in our lives requires discernment and sensitivity. In some cases, our sharing may bless the other person and draw him or her to Christ or to a deeper experience of Him; on the other hand, in some cases we need to heed Jesus' warning:

> "Do not give what is holy to the dogs; nor cast your pearls before swine, lest they trample them under their feet, and turn and tear you to pieces."[2]

Now, obviously, Jesus is speaking metaphorically here. What is "holy" is not for those who disdain and repudiate it, according to our Lord. Our pearls, the precious moments with Him, "pearls of wisdom" that we receive from the Word (which some folks may not even have the capacity to understand, much less appreciate), and other spiritual insights, are not always for anyone and everyone. Jesus warned that some may trample it and turn on us, verbally or physically destroying us. What is particularly disheartening is to see that "dogs" can thrive even in churches; they are not exclusive to the outside world. We live in such an ungodly culture these days that even the church has been tainted, as have some of the seminaries and other religious institutions.

> *Many years ago, a prominent theologian and professor at a faithful seminary gave a litmus test for cults: "What do they say about Jesus Christ?"*

Many years ago, a prominent theologian and professor at a faithful seminary gave a litmus test for cults: "What do they say about Jesus Christ?" Today, that same litmus test can be applied to other areas – what do they say about His death? About His Resurrection? About His second advent? This is a test for whether

---

[2] Matthew 7:6

we are in a place where it is safe to share that which is "holy" or in a place where what we have been given as "pearls" is not welcome. It calls for great discernment and reliance on the still, quiet voice of the Holy Spirit to know when, where, and how we should share what Jesus Christ has done for us.

We must also be very careful about giving people instructions, especially if we are using Biblical stories to make a point, and we must be very careful about allowing someone else to tell us what we are to do in a given situation. How often have we heard someone say, "God told me that *you* are to…." as if the Holy Spirit is incapable of communicating with the person involved. This is not to say that we cannot get good advice and counsel from others, but if it goes against that "still quiet voice," we had better be quite discerning. The enemy can speak through the most sincere, well-meaning people (including *us*!). We have a prime example in the life of Peter. No sooner had he pronounced the great statement of faith, "You are the Christ, the Son of the living God" in answer to Jesus' question, "But who do you say that I am?" and been told he would be given "the keys of the kingdom of heaven" than Jesus rebuked him severely:

> From that time Jesus began to show His disciples that He must go to Jerusalem, and suffer many things from the elders and chief priests and scribes, and be killed, and be raised the third day. Then Peter took Him aside and began to rebuke Him, saying, "Far be it from You Lord; this shall not happen to You!"
>
> But He turned and said to Peter, "*Get behind Me Satan*! You are an offense to Me, for you are not mindful of the things of God, but the things of men."[3]

---

[3] Matthew 16:21-23; italics added

What? Satan? Wasn't it Peter who was speaking? Yes, but the source of the response to Jesus' warning was the enemy, and he spoke through Peter. What a warning for all of us. Sincerity and concern are no marks of speaking on behalf of God. Jesus makes a distinction that must be another plumb line: the difference between the things of God and the things of men. We must be mindful that we are concerned with the things of God.

Are we listening? Are we receiving? Are we discerning, so that we know when and when not to share what God is giving us?

Send It: The Recipients

John was told to send the message: "to the seven churches which are in Asia: to Ephesus, to Smyrna, to Pergamos, to Thyatira, to Sardis, to Philadelphia, and to Laodicea."[4] The order of the towns corresponds to their geographical arrangement and was the usual route that would have been taken by a courier delivering the messages.

We have already looked briefly at the recipients with regard to the "angels" of the churches, but there are a few other considerations. For instance, the number may or may not have symbolic relevance. Because of the apocalyptic nature of the book, it likely does, and so we will consider some of the possible symbolic implications.

In symbolism in the Scriptures, the number "7" often is considered to represent completeness or wholeness. It occurs numerous times in the Old Testament, beginning with the seven days of creation, with God resting on the seventh day, having declared everything "good." According to the Law, man was to refrain from work on the Sabbath, or seventh day of the week, and the year of Jubilee followed seven times seven years.[5] The Feast of

---

[4] Revelation 1:11
[5] Leviticus 25:8

Unleavened Bread and the Feast of Tabernacles lasted seven days,[6] and the Day of Atonement occurred in the seventh month.

A notable instance is the use in the account of Jericho: Joshua and the seven primary priests marched around the walls of Jericho for seven days, blowing seven trumpets, before the walls collapsed. The tabernacle was dedicated on the seventh day[7] and had seven types or classes of furniture (bronze altar, bronze laver, golden lampstand, table of showbread, altar of incense, ark of the covenant, and the mercy seat). The lampstand in the holy place of the tabernacle was symbolic of Jesus as the "Light of the world" and had seven branches – a central shaft with six branches, three on either side – and seven cup-shaped lamps for the oil (symbolic of the Holy Spirit).

The number also is prevalent in the Gospels. We have Jesus giving seven parables of the Kingdom in Matthew 13 and pronouncing seven woes on the Pharisees in Matthew 23. In Mark 8, we have the story of Jesus feeding 4,000 people from seven loaves and a few fish, after which seven basketfuls were collected. Luke recorded that Mary Magdalene was possessed by seven demons,[8] and John presented seven signs and seven "I Am" statements in his gospel.

The number is especially prevalent in Revelation, where it occurs some 54 times; there are seven churches, seven angels to the seven churches, a Lamb with seven horns and seven eyes, seven Spirits of God, seven seals, seven trumpets, seven trumpet plagues, seven thunders, and seven last plagues. The dragon and the beast have seven heads. The first resurrection occurs at the seventh trumpet. We will consider a few of these instances when we get to John's vision of the glorified Lord.

If we consider that seven has some sense of completeness, and especially if we consider its use in the furniture in the tabernacle,

---

[6] Exodus 12:15, 19; Numbers 29:12
[7] Exodus 40:17
[8] Luke 8:2

all of which is symbolic of Jesus Christ, then we can consider the letters and the subsequent prophecy to be the risen and glorified Jesus Christ's message to the entire Church. For now, we need to be concerned only with realizing that Jesus Christ has a special message for each person.

Are we ready to listen?
Are we willing to obey?

ONE LIKE THE SON OF MAN

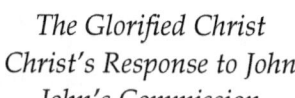

The Glorified Christ
Christ's Response to John
John's Commission

Then I turned to see the voice that spoke with me. And having turned I saw seven golden lampstands, and in the midst of the seven lampstands One like the Son of Man, clothed with a garment down to the feet and girded about the chest with a golden band. His head and hair were white like wool, as white as snow, and His eyes like a flame of fire; His feet were like fine brass, as if refined in a furnace, and His voice as the sound of many waters; He had in His right hand seven stars, out of His mouth went a sharp two-edged sword, and His countenance was like the sun shining in its strength.
And when I saw Him, I fell at His feet as dead. But He laid His right hand on me, saying to me, "Do not be afraid; I am the First and the Last. I am He who lives, and was dead, and behold, I am alive forevermore. Amen. And I have the keys of Hades and of Death.
Write the things which you have seen, and the things which are, and the things which will take place after this. The mystery of the seven stars which you saw in My right hand, and the seven golden lampstands: The seven stars are the angels of the seven churches, and the seven lampstands which you saw are the seven churches. (Revelation 1:12-20)

CHAPTER EIGHT

The Glorified Christ

Then I turned to see the voice that spoke with me. And having turned I saw seven golden lampstands, and in the midst of the seven lampstands One like the Son of Man, clothed with a garment down to the feet and girded about the chest with a golden band. His head and hair were white like wool, as white as snow, and His eyes like a flame of fire; His feet were like fine brass, as if refined in a furnace, and His voice as the sound of many waters; He had in His right hand seven stars, out of His mouth went a sharp two-edged sword, and His countenance was like the sun shining in its strength.

John turned to see the source of the voice . . . and dropped to his knees. The description he offers of the One standing before him is highly symbolic. It is an astonishing sight, and John relates the incident in three stages: what he saw, his reaction, and Christ's response. Each of these aspects has important implications for us. John's description of this awesome sight is a masterpiece of symbolic artistry.

A Figure Appears

He saw seven golden lampstands, and in their midst a figure of "One like the Son of Man." The seven golden lampstands represent seven churches, as we will learn later (1:20).

The Lampstands

The lampstands evoke images of the golden lampstand described in Exodus for use in the tabernacle:

> "make a lampstand of pure gold; the lampstand shall be of hammered work. Its shaft, its branches, its bowls, its ornamental knobs, and flowers shall be of one piece. And six branches shall come out of

its side: three branches . . . out of one side, and three branches . . . out of the other side . . . . You shall make seven lamps for it, and they shall arrange its lamps so that they give light in front of it."[1]

The significance of the symbol is found in its purpose: the lampstand itself is not light but sheds light on those around it. Hence, the seven lampstands, as representatives of the seven churches, suggest that the churches' principal function is to give forth light. This is consistent with the typological reading of this lampstand, which is quite common: it represents the Lord Jesus Christ – the gold, His deity and glory, and the hammered work His humanity and crucifixion – as the "Light of the world."[2] As that Light, He told his disciples and *us* that we are to shed His light upon a dark world:

> "You are the light of the world. A city that is set on a hill cannot be hidden. Nor do they light a lamp and put it under a basket, but on a lampstand, and it gives light to all *who are* in the house. Let your light so shine before men, that they may see your good works and glorify your Father in heaven."[3]

The questions for each of us are:

> *Are we shining the light of Jesus before men and women and children? Do they see our good works? Do they glorify our Father in heaven?*

---

[1] Exodus 25:31, 32, 37; see also Zechariah 4
[2] John 8:12, 9:5
[3] Matthew 5:14-16

Standing in the midst of the lampstands was One clothed with a garment girded with a golden band, with head and hair white as wool or snow, with eyes like a flame of fire, feet like fine brass, and a voice as the sound of many waters. A full study of this figure with its symbolic explanations is an amazing and rewarding study. We will look only briefly at the implications, but I encourage the reader to explore this symbolism more deeply.

His Garment

First of all, the garment reached to the feet and is girded with a golden band. It was much like the long garment worn by the High Priest of the Old Testament. So, in this sense, the figure was one of priestly order, indeed, a High Priest. Clearly, it is meant to demonstrate what the writer to the Hebrews tells us concerning Jesus Christ:

> *who is* holy, harmless, undefiled, separate from sinners, and has become higher than the heavens; who does not need daily, as those high priests, to offer up sacrifices, first for His own sins and then for the people's, for this He did once for all when He offered up Himself. But He, because He continues forever, has an *unchangeable priesthood*. Therefore He is also able to save to the uttermost those who come to God through Him, since He always lives to make intercession for them.[4]
>
> . . . .
>
> Seeing then that we have *a great High Priest* who has passed through the heavens, Jesus the Son of God, let us hold fast *our* confession. For we do not have a High Priest who cannot sympathize with our weaknesses, but was in all *points* tempted as *we are, yet* without sin. Let us therefore come boldly to

---

[4] Hebrews 7:26, 27; 7:24, 25; italics added

the throne of grace, that we may obtain mercy and find grace to help in time of need.[5]

The importance of Jesus as our High Priest cannot be overstated. As Gordon Borden has said,

> The priestly ministry of Jesus Christ is at the heart of the doctrine of salvation. The essence of the Christian faith is found in the twofold aspect of Christ's priesthood, in the incarnation in which he took on our human nature and in the offering of Himself to God the Father on our behalf. As the Son of God, Christ is both fully human and fully divine. In the opening sentence of the Gospel of John, we see echoed the opening phrases of Genesis: "In the beginning was the Word, and the Word was with God, and the Word was God" and then we are told that "the Word became flesh and dwelt among us, and we have seen his glory, glory as of the only son from the Father."[6] The faith of the Church rests on the singular priesthood of Christ, thus presupposing the incarnation and the doctrine of the Trinity.[7]

What does this mean to *us*? Jesus Christ is holy; He is undefiled; He is separate from sinners (being without sin); and He is higher than the heavens. As such, He has paid for *our* sins – once, for all – with His blood. He saves us, and He makes intercession for us. Isn't that an amazing thought? Jesus Christ right now is praying for *you*! For *me*! He interposes His blood; when the enemy accuses us before the Father, Jesus Christ presents His blood. Further, He understands our weaknesses; He does not judge us – rather He understands, is compassionate, and makes a way of escape. He

---

[5] Hebrews 4:14-16
[6] John 1:1,14
[7] Borden, Gordon. *A Theological Journey: insights on the faith once delivered.* Ekklesia Society Publications, 2016, p. 93

ever lives to make intercession for us. In all, He loves us, as the Father loves Him!

The great hymn by Robert Robinson puts it this way:

> Jesus sought me when a stranger,
> Wandering from the fold of God;
> He, to rescue me from danger,
> Interposed His precious blood;
> How His kindness yet pursues me
> Mortal tongue can never tell,
> Clothed in flesh, till death shall loose me
> I cannot proclaim it well.[8]

Amazing grace, indeed. As if that were not enough, our great High Priest bids us to "come boldly before the throne of grace to receive mercy in time of need."[9] We proclaim with the words of yet another hymn, "Hallelujah, what a Savior!"[10]

Do we really believe (in other words, live our lives based on the truth) that Jesus not only bids us, but actually commands us, to come boldly?

His Physical Appearance

After describing the lampstands, the garment, and Christ's position among them, John paints a portrait of His different physical characteristics using various similes, as noted above. Gros Louis notes that, "This . . . portrait is also another indicator of the artistic unity of the revelations, for the characteristics of Christ enumerated here will reappear in the seven letters."[11]

---

[8] Robinson, Robert. "Come, Thou Fount of Every Blessing," *A Collection of Hymns used by the Church of Christ in Angel Alley, Bishopgate*, 1759
[9] Hebrews 4:16
[10] Bliss, Philip P. "Hallelujah! What a Savior." *International Lessons Monthly*, 1875.
[11] Gros 334

A brief summary is sufficient:

(1) His head and feet, white as wool and snow, symbolize His *purity and holiness*;
(2) His eyes, "like a flame of fire," denote *fierce judgment*;
(3) His feet, "like fine brass, as if refined in a furnace," symbolize *His strength or power to crush*, done in righteousness to justify His holiness;
(4) His voice, like "the sound of many waters," sings *the glory and majesty of God*;
(5) His right hand, holding "seven stars," demonstrates His *omnipotence and protection*;
(6) His mouth, from which comes a "sharp two-edged sword," speaks of the *power of His word* and that He penetrates our deepest thoughts and attitudes[12]; and
(7) His face, "like the sun shining in its strength," reflects *Christ's Resurrection glory*.

John's Reaction

At the sight, John "fell to his feet as dead" (1:17). His response is much like that of Moses, who "hid his face, for he was afraid to look upon God,"[13] or the prophet Isaiah, who was so overcome by his own condition when confronted by the vision of the holiness of God, that he cried out,

> "Woe is me! For I am lost; for I am a man of unclean lips, and I dwell in the midst of a people of unclean lips; for my eyes have seen the King, the Lord of hosts!"[14]

It is similar to Thomas' response upon seeing the risen Christ for the first time.

---

[12] Hebrews 4:12
[13] Exodus 3:6
[14] Isaiah 6:5

We should pause and ponder these responses. Some of these instances occurred in the Old Testament, before Jesus Christ walked upon the earth and called his disciples "friends." This is an interesting distinction that many people misunderstand and use to reinvent a god of their own liking – to create a Jesus-buddy that is merely a figment of their imaginations and then propose to worship this idol in what actually constitutes a dreadfully misguided concept if not downright heresy. Sadly, it happens every Sunday in churches across the country and around the world. People gather to engage in an exercise ranging from indifference toward the holiness of God to a frenzy of emotion-charged entertainment and activity that has little, if anything, to do with true worship – in spirit and in truth.[15]

> *I am reminded of our one instance of attending a local huge megachurch (intended redundancy) several years ago. My "adopted" mama was visiting from out of state and immediately upon arriving stated that she wanted to attend that gathering on Sunday morning because she and her friends had heard all about it. My husband, a staunch Anglican, would have nothing of it. For a week, they bantered back and forth: she pleaded, he gently but firmly refused. Sunday morning arrived, and as we were getting dressed, I finally convinced him that he would not go to hell if he acquiesced to the desires of an 84-year-old Baptist and took her to the megachurch. We arrived early, so we were able to get prime seating in the huge auditorium (no resemblance to a church) – first row in the "mezzanine."*
>
> *The event began! Strobe lights and loud music gave way to swinging and dancing and jumping up-and-down. I watched the Anglican stiffness oozing from my husband's pores! Then it happened! He spotted the TV cameras and FROZE, wide-eyed and horrified. He turned to me and said, "They have cameras – someone*

---

[15] John 4:24

might see me here!" I reassured him: "Believe me, someone in the sound room has already contacted the cameramen and told them when they pan the audience to make sure they avoid capturing the look on the face of the guy with the beard in the suit!"

Then my sweet little "mama," leaned over and whispered, "If he wants to go to your church, we can leave now and still get there, can't we?" I leaned the other way and 'forwarded' the message to my husband, who promptly responded, "Nope! She wanted to come here; we're going to stay for the entire performance!" And, so we did.

When we got home, "mama" promptly went to the computer to get more information on the pastor and the church and then let out a gasp: "They don't even have a cross in the building!"

No, they don't – in fact, they have a very large globe on the stage instead. For me, it was a metaphor of what had happened there and happens so often: they had replaced the cross with the world. Was that worship? I don't question what other people were experiencing, but for us, it was little more than a rock concert. We are better served by looking at the instances recorded in Scripture to get a genuine concept of worship.

Isaiah, as an example, realized the sin inherent in his humanity, that distinction that "all have sinned and fallen short of the glory of God."[16] He cried out, "Woe is me!" Is this not ultimately the cry of all of us who have confronted our sins? Then, "I am lost" – therein lies the acknowledgment of one's need for Jesus Christ.

Those words have echoed down the centuries and are captured in the well-known hymn by John Newton:

---

[16] Romans 3:23

> Amazing Grace, how sweet the sound,
> That saved a wretch like me.
> *I once was lost* but now am found,
> Was blind, but now I see.[17]

In the New Testament, we have a great example in Thomas, a disciple who had been with the Lord Jesus for the three years of His ministry but had seen his hopes of being prominent in the Messiah's kingdom dashed to pieces when Jesus Christ was arrested, tried (of sorts), and crucified. He was not even with the other disciples when Jesus Christ first appeared to them. He certainly wasn't about to believe what this group had to say about seeing a dead man now alive again! What nonsense, he might have said. Indeed, he said as much, "Unless I see in His hands the print of the nails, and put my finger into the print of the nails, and put my hand into His side, I will not believe."[18]

> *He [Thomas] certainly wasn't about to believe what this group had to say about seeing a dead man now alive again!*

I've always thought Thomas has gotten a really bad rap – most preachers come down really hard on him, but I can't be so critical of him – for goodness sakes, he didn't have the New Testament to read, and if we fault him for failing to recognize what Jesus had prepared for him to know, then the whole motley group should be included: if we compare the two events – Jesus with the disciples in the upper room and then again with them when Thomas was present – we find almost identical words spoken.

The difference in response is what is astounding: Thomas fell at Jesus' feet (no record that any of the others did – so much for "doubting" Thomas!), much as Isaiah had done centuries earlier. His cry is every bit as incriminating of his own sin and glorifying of the One who bid him come: "My Lord and My God!"

---

[17] Newton, John. "Amazing Grace." Italics added
[18] John 20:25b

We come, then, to John's response. It seems redundant to describe it – have we not seen the reaction already in Isaiah's and Thomas' responses? Indeed, we have, for John, too, "fell at His feet as dead." "Woe is me!" "My Lord and my God!"

These are the scriptural reactions to confrontations with the Holy One. How they differ from the casual attitude or chaotic carrying-on that passes itself as "praising" God! The One who said, "you are My friends" stands in all His glory before John, and instinctively John falls at His feet as dead. He may be our Friend – indeed, "what a Friend we have in Jesus" – and He may be our "brother," but He has never ceased to be God – God incarnate, yes, but no less pure, holy, glorious.

Have we fallen at His feet?
If not, we have not gotten a true grasp of Him.

CHAPTER NINE

Christ's Response to John

But He laid His right hand on me, saying to me, "Do not be afraid; I am the First and the Last. I am He who lives, and was dead, and behold, I am alive forevermore. Amen. And I have the keys of Hades and of Death.

But . . . . How what follows this word can change everything, including the course of history! Its rather like "if," noted by someone as the largest two-letter word in the English language.

The Touch

John says, " "But, He laid His right hand on me, . . ." John tells us what Jesus Christ said, but before we look at His words, we should pause again and consider the implications associated with this phrase. Among them are two: the response to John's reaction and the personal touch, both of which speak volumes concerning our Lord's presence in *our* lives. John clearly was frightened and, as with Isaiah and Thomas, our earlier examples, God moved to make the encounter intensely personal. In Isaiah's case, one of the seraphim took a coal from the fire, placed it on Isaiah's lips, and told him that his iniquity was taken away and his sin purged. In Thomas' encounter, Jesus appeared and offered his hands and his side for Thomas to inspect. Another instance is Daniel's experience after receiving a vision, which he describes thus:

> Now, as he was speaking with me, I was in a deep sleep with my face to the ground; but he touched me, and stood me upright. And he said, "Look, I am making known to you what shall happen in the latter time of the indignation; for at the appointed time the end shall be."[1]

---

[1] Daniel 8:18, 19

So, too, with John, the Lord responded, first to John's fear with a very personal gesture. So, too, with us, for the Lord Jesus knows all our emotions and situations and meets us at the very point of our need. Swete makes an interesting observation, namely that the fact that Christ's hand holds seven stars

> Does not hinder it from being laid on the Seer, for the whole representation is symbol and art. The Hand which sustains Nature and the Churches at the same time quickens and raises individual lives.[2]

What an astounding truth: the One who holds the universe together stoops to be involved in *your* life and *my* life.

Further, the touch of His *right* hand is representative of power and authority. The right hand symbolically is associated with salvation, refuge, protection (Psalm 16:8), and judgment (119:1; Jer 22:24), as well as with a favored position. It is from the position at God's right hand that Jesus Christ intercedes as our High Priest (Mark 16:19; Acts 2:33; Rom 8:34; Hebrews 1:3; Heb 8:1) and exercises authority over all powers (I Peter 3:22).[3]

Seven Words

Having touched John, the glorified Lord Jesus speaks to him, first to comfort, then to emphasize His power, and finally to give John a commission. In each aspect of this encounter, we find truths relevant to our own lives.

---

[2] Swete, p. 19
[3] For more information on hand and right hand, consult Elwell, Walter A. *Evangelical Dictionary of Theology*, 1997.

"Fear not"

Jesus spoke. "Do not be afraid," He said. Christ's exhortation to "not be afraid" echoes many instances in the Old Testament when God encouraged His servants to maintain an eternal perspective and to rely upon Him. It is particularly reminiscent of God's encouragement to Jeremiah. Prior to commissioning Jeremiah, God told him not to be afraid and

> Then the Lord put forth His hand and touched [his] mouth, and the Lord said to [him]: "Behold, I have put My words in your mouth. See, I have this day set you over the nations and over the kingdoms."[4]

John undoubtedly would have been familiar with this and other Old Testament occurrences. His inclusion of these moments with the risen Lord helps to establish and authenticate the divine nature of the revelation.

In other instances, Jesus said the same words: "Fear not," or words to that effect. We are reminded, of course, of the instance when Jesus was on the boat with the disciples and had fallen asleep. Suddenly, a tempest arose and the boat was tossed about, being covered with waves. The disciples finally awakened Jesus, saying, "Lord, save us! We are perishing!" His response? "Why are you fearful, O you of little faith?" Then he arose and rebuked the winds and the sea, after which everything was calm. The men marveled.[5]

We need not be fearful, either, for the same Lord, who has mastery over nature, cares for us as well.

In another instance, Jesus sent the disciples out on the sea to go to the other side, after He had fed the multitudes and needed some time alone. Later, he walked across the sea, but as He approached the boat, they saw Him and thought it was a ghost – and "they

---

[4] Jeremiah 1:9, 10.
[5] Matthew 8:23-27

cried out for fear." Jesus immediately spoke words of comfort to them, "Be of good cheer! It is I; do not be afraid."[6] In the midst of every circumstance that might cause us to fear, Jesus comes and says, "do not be afraid." And, finally, we have the comforting words, this time from Luke, when Jesus said,

> "Are not five sparrows sold for two copper coins? And not one of them is forgotten before God. But the very hairs of your head are all numbered. *Do not fear therefore*; you are of more value than many sparrows.[7]

Six "I Am" Statements

In identifying Himself to John, Christ used a combination of six terms to describe Himself. Rhetorically, they form two triadic (remember the earlier instances of the use of three, as with the Trinity?) structures. He is (1) the first, (2) the last, and (3) He who lives, also translated "the living One' and, then, (a) was dead, and (b) is alive, and (c) has the keys of Hades and of Death.

First Triad

The first triad reinforces the statement of His eternal existence and sovereign power. The first two terms (first, last) echo terms used, for example, in Isaiah:

> "Thus says the Lord, the King of Israel,
> And his Redeemer, the Lord of hosts:
> 'I am the First and I am the Last;
> Besides Me there is no God.'"[8]

---

[6] Matthew 14:25-27
[7] Luke 12:6; italics added
[8] Isaiah 44:6

And, again

> "Listen to Me, O Jacob,
> And Israel, My called:
> I am He, I am the First,
> I am also the Last.
> Indeed My hand has laid the foundation of the earth,
> And My right hand has stretched the heavens;
> When I call to them,
> They stand up together."[9]

The third term, "the One who lives" or "the living One," also echoes Old Testament self-descriptions of God, one of which is a statement that Joshua made to the people of Israel after the Lord had given him instructions for moving forward: "So Joshua said to the children of Israel, 'Come here, and hear the words of the Lord your God.' And Joshua said, 'By this you shall know that the *living God* is among you . . .'"[10]

> *The emphasis on "living" sets the God of Israel apart from the dead and inanimate gods of other religions.*

And He still is today! He is among us! He is in us! He goes before us, and He comes behind us, and He walks beside us!

The emphasis on "living" sets the God of Israel apart from the dead and inanimate gods of other religions. In using the term, the risen Christ substantiated His immutability, emphasizing that the Triune God is consistent in His character and in His revelation of Himself to the human race. It reminds us of Paul's words to the Church in Colossae

> He is the image of the invisible God, the firstborn over all creation. For by Him all things were

---

[9] Isaiah 48: 12, 13
[10] Joshua 3:9, 10, italics added

created that are in heaven and that are on earth, visible and invisible, whether thrones or dominions or principalities or powers. All things were created through Him and for Him. And He is before all things, and in Him all things consist. And He is the head of the body, the church, who is the beginning, the firstborn from the dead, that in all things He may have the preeminence.[11]

This is the One who loves us and calls us to Himself.

Second Triad

The second triad shifts the focus from Christ's person to His work. The use of polysyndeton (conjunctions between each word or phrase in a series) is a rhetorical technique that sets off each item in a series as being especially important. In this case, the work involves His death (was dead) *and* His Resurrection ("and behold, I am alive forever more) *and* His authority ("I have the keys of Hades and of Death").

> *So, God in Christ entered this world, took on human form, and took your place and mine in death.*

First is His death: the Cross of Calvary, whereon the Son of God shed His blood for "without the shedding of blood there is no remission for sin," whereon He died in *your* place and *mine*, whereon He "became sin that we might become the righteousness of God in Him." This is the beginning of the Gospel! This is the beginning of the Good News! God so loved the world that He sent His only begotten Son, that whosoever believes in Him *should not perish* but have everlasting life.[12] By implication, those who do *not* believe in Him *are perishing*.

---

[11] Colossians 1:15-18
[12] John 3:16

So, God in Christ entered this world, took on human form, and took your place and mine in death, for since that fateful day in the Garden, when Adam and Eve opted to believe the lie that their disobedience would not result in death and acted accordingly,[13] all humanity has entered the world spiritually dead. This is a heavy theological point but one that must be acknowledged if we are to "have everlasting life." Paul described it this way:

> And you He made alive, who were dead in trespasses and sins, in which you once walked according to the course of this world, according to the prince of the power of the air, the spirit who now works in the sons of disobedience, among whom also we all once conducted ourselves in the lusts of our flesh, fulfilling the desires of the flesh and of the mind, and *were by nature children of wrath*, just as the others. [14]

That death came from sin: disobeying God. Sin manifests in many fashions and sizes, and we are often tempted to categorize sin or overlay a human grading system on it, but the reality is that sin is sin, and that every sin put Jesus on the cross.

One question that I ask when someone wants to assume a superior situation to someone else is: "What sin did *not* put Jesus on the cross?" At the foot of the Cross, we all come in our fallen state to receive mercy and salvation; at the foot of the cross we realize the price that was paid in full by His suffering on our behalf, by His shed blood, by His separation from the Father in that hour when He cried, "My God, my God, why have you forsaken Me?"

If we think that we are less "sinful" than someone else and exalt ourselves accordingly, we have merely fallen for a more subtle sin, namely pride, and it was pride that caused Lucifer to rise up against God in the first place – in other words, we have become as

---

[13] Genesis 3
[14] Ephesians 2:1-3 (emphasis mine)

the enemy in our self-righteousness. The truth of Scripture is that "there is none righteous, no, not one."[15]

Further, if we accept the attitude that is so prevalent today, which says that sin is a human construct to make people feel guilty and that we are not sinners, we have fallen for yet another lie:

> If we say that *we have no sin, we deceive ourselves,* and *the truth is not in us.* If we confess our sins, He is faithful and just to forgive us *our* sins and to cleanse us from all unrighteousness. If we say that we have not sinned, *we make Him a liar,* and *His word is not in us.*[16]

This is powerful! Look at the four consequences of saying that we have no sin:
- we deceive ourselves
- the truth is not in us
- we make Him a liar
- His word is not in us.

We could elaborate on each of these four points, but an explication of those verses must be saved for another time. Nonetheless, you are encouraged to stop and meditate on each point. Notice how this description aligns with the "fall" in the Garden. Nothing is new; the enemy is still deceiving, and the truth still escapes us if we do not take God at His word.

One interesting note, which gets a bit theological but is an important aside, is that the better translation of the first term is rendered by the NASB: "became dead." Maclaren explains why this difference in verb tenses is important:

> The language of the original is, perhaps, scarcely capable of smooth transference into English . . . what is said is not 'I *was* dead,' as describing a past

---

[15] Romans 3:10
[16] I John 1:8-10 (emphasis mine)

condition, but "I *became* dead,' as describing a past act . . . . The only possibility of death, for 'the Living One,' lies in His enwrapping Himself with that which can die . . . . It is very significant that the same word . . . describe[s] the same Lord's incarnation: 'The Word became flesh,' and so the Life 'became dead.'[17]

Second, just as the "Word became flesh" and the Life "became dead," so the dead One "became alive ever more"! Death could not hold Him! That which had reigned since the Garden, which kept men and women in a prison of fear, was defeated on Calvary.

> *That which had reigned since the Garden, which kept men and women in a prison of fear, was defeated on Calvary.*

Peter, in his first sermon, delivered on the day of Pentecost, explained that David's prophecy ("For You will not leave my soul in Hades, Nor will You allow Your Holy One to see corruption") had been fulfilled by Jesus Christ:

> "Therefore, being a prophet, and knowing that God had sworn with an oath to him that of the fruit of his body, according to the flesh, He would raise up the Christ to sit on the throne, he foreseeing this, spoke concerning the resurrection of the Christ, that His soul was not left in Hades, nor did His flesh see corruption. This Jesus God has raised up, of which we are all witnesses."[18]

"I am alive ever more," Jesus said. Jesus Christ conquered death. Death is no more for the one who is in Him.

Further, in appearing to His disciples after the Resurrection and before His ascension to the Father and to the glory that He had

---

[17] Maclaren, p. 165
[18] Acts 2: 26, 30-32

shared with the Father from eternity to His incarnation, He told them that

> "All authority has been given to Me in heaven and on earth. Go therefore and make disciples of all the nations, baptizing them in the name of the Father and of the Son and of the Holy Spirit, teaching them to observe all things that I have commanded you; and lo, I am with you always, *even* to the end of the age." Amen.

How do we do that? In His power, and in His name. He did not leave us alone, and He did not leave us in our sin. Rather, He made us alive in Him:

> But God, who is rich in mercy, because of His great love with which He loved us, even when we were dead in trespasses, *made us alive together with Christ* (by grace you have been saved), and raised *us* up together, and made *us* sit together in the heavenly *places* in Christ Jesus, that in the ages to come He might show the exceeding riches of His grace in *His kindness toward us in Christ Jesus*. For by grace you have been saved through faith, and that not of yourselves; *it is* the gift of God, not of works, lest anyone should boast.[19]

The emphasis, then, is on the Resurrection, for the implication is that Christ did not merely reenter the realm from "whence he had come; he entered a new life in which death has been conquered forever."[20] What a glorious truth this phrase has for us. Death is conquered; death is no more.

> *Death is conquered;*
> *death is no more.*

---

[19] Ephesians 2:4-9, italics added
[20] Ladd, p. 34

The *third* phrase emphasizes this point: He has "the keys of Hades and of Death." The term "keys" is symbolic of authority, suggesting one's ability to enter a domain at will and to have access to every portion of it. The term *Hades* is the Greek equivalent for *Sheol* of the Old Testament and refers to the place of all the departed dead (see Acts 2:27, 31) or the place appointed for the departed wicked (see Luke 16:23 and Revelation 20:13, 14).

The point is that Christ declared His authority over those confined in Hades, as well as over those who are with him in "Paradise." In addition, He is Master over death, having "robbed death of its sting, satan of his power, the grave of its victory." Paul put it this way:

> So when this corruptible has put on incorruption, and this mortal has put on immortality, then shall be brought to pass the saying that is written: "Death is swallowed up in victory."
> "O Death, where *is* your sting?
> O Hades, where *is* your victory?"
> The sting of death *is* sin, and the strength of sin *is* the law. But thanks *be* to God, who gives us the victory through our Lord Jesus Christ.[21]

Pauls' exhortation is also for us: "be steadfast, immovable, always abounding in the work of the Lord, knowing that your labor is not in vain in the Lord."

How are we doing?

---

[21] I Corinthians 15: 54-57

CHAPTER TEN

John's Commission

*Write the things which you have seen, and the things which are,
and the things which will take place after this. The mystery of the seven stars
which you saw in My right hand, and the seven golden lampstands:
The seven stars are the angels of the seven churches,
and the seven lampstands which you saw are the seven churches.*

Christ had completed His identification, so clearly consistent with instances in the Old Testament when God appeared to an individual and gave him or her instructions. It was time now for John's commission, which was to write down what he had seen, what is, and what would occur at a later date: past, present, future – yet another triad!

Christ's Explanation

Christ then explained the symbolic meaning of His appearance among the candlesticks. This explanation is important, especially for literary purposes, because it establishes and confirms the viability of recognizing that certain portions of this text are symbolic of something else.

In this case, the stars represent the "angels" of the seven churches, Christ said. No explanation accompanies the statement. Elsewhere in Scripture, "angels" refers to both supernatural beings and simple messengers. Various interpretations are given, one of which suggests that the term, which means *messenger*, refers to the pastor or priest, the one who would be the "messenger" to the entire gathering. Another interpretation suggests that each church is assigned an angel that protects and guards it, which poses a bit of a problem when we get to the individual letters, where the message is clearly sent to the leader of the church.

We are not so concerned here with the meaning of the word as with the power and authority that Jesus Christ has over the Church: He is the Head of the Church, and He had a message for it – and still does. He holds the "stars" in His right hand, meaning that He exercises all authority and judgment over them, and all the "angels" ultimately answer to Him.

One wonders today how many holding leadership positions in the Church realize the impact of this message on their own lives and ministries. Certainly, Christ's Church has many faithful, devoted, and caring "angels," but the instances of abuse and other forms of damage that have been perpetrated on Christ's sheep by His so-called "under-shepherds" are astounding and heartbreaking at best. The stories of sexual abuse shock and horrify us, as well they should. These are obvious instances of deliberate defilement of the very call to ordination, but the abuse can also be verbal or exhibited in numerous other ways. I think especially of one dear faithful believer who was so wounded by the verbal attack of her "angel" that even years later she will not entertain ever again taking a leadership position.

Wounded child of God – wounded by the "angel" of that church. She has recovered beautifully, as her confidence is in the Lord Jesus Christ. Were this an isolated incident, one might tend to question this person's story, but other similar ones happened in this particular environment. The tragedy is that this is just one of so many instances throughout the Church, regardless of denomination, some deliberate like this one, and some totally unintentional. Jesus Christ holds these "angels" in His right hand of authority.

We should be praying for all of them!
What a responsibility they have!

Jesus Christ's Presence in the Church

The "seven lampstands" are the seven churches, Jesus Christ said, and from this explanation, we can see that the picture of Him standing in their midst is symbolic of His presence at the center of the Church universal. In the midst of local churches that had some distinct problems, as evident in the seven letters, is the ever faithful Head, the Good Shepherd among His straying sheep. As we consider that He was sending a message to the "angels" of the churches, we are reminded that He charged them to care for His sheep as under-shepherds.

> *I will never again hear the passage of Peter's restoration without remembering the point that the Lord drove home during the sermon and charge given to me at my own ordination. As the speaker, a friend and then president of the seminary, spoke on Jesus telling Peter to feed His lambs, tend His sheep, feed His sheep,[1] a passage that is familiar to almost everyone and one that I had preached on myself, suddenly the emphasis changed completely. Prior to that moment, I had always concentrated on the verbs: feed, tend, feed. However, as he spoke, I heard "another voice" saying My, My, My . . . feed MY lambs, tend MY sheep, feed MY sheep – never forget they are MINE! My prayer is that I never forget! May none of us ever forget to Whom they belong.*

Further, even in writing this portion, I am reminded of a little lamb a friend gave me years ago (I use to collect stuffed lambs). On the lamb's underbody, she had pinned a piece of paper saying, "Remember Whose you are!" Those words have carried me through many trials and hardships. "Remember Whose you are!" So, it works both ways.

Remember, they are HIS lambs, HIS sheep...
Remember Whose YOU are!

---

[1] John 21:15-17

AFTERWORD

We have looked at a chapter of Scripture that receives little attention. For the most part, studies of Revelation focus on the letters to the seven churches or on the prophecy of future events, or perhaps both. The first chapter often is treated as merely preliminary to more exciting or relevant things, and yet what can possibly be more exciting and relevant than a glimpse of the crucified, risen, and *glorified* Lord Jesus Christ?

This book is a meager attempt to explore some of what John recorded in his initial encounter. Every word is important! The description of Jesus Christ, John's immediate response (indicative of the Lord's awesome holiness, purity, and glory), and Jesus' gentle, personal response, as well as His commission, have great significance for each of us who claim to be His disciples. Hence, the author invites you to join in learning more of Him as we journey Home, to the Bridegroom. May each of us be more conscious that we are commissioned to live as His betrothed, as lights in a dark world giving testimony in everything we say and do to the reality that He has redeemed us as His own, so that others, too, might seek Him.

Hebrews 13:20, 21

NOTES:

www.ingramcontent.com/pod-product-compliance
Lightning Source LLC
Chambersburg PA
CBHW060200050426
42446CB00013B/2918